Sarah Flower, a leading nutritionist and author of many cookery books, is passionate about healthy eating and is a keen advocate of the sugar-free and low-carb way of eating. Sarah writes for a number of publications, including the *Daily Mail*, *Top Santé* magazine and *Healthista*. She appears regularly on BBC Radio Devon.

The Everyday Family Air Fryer Cookbook

Delicious, Quick and Easy Recipes for Busy Families
Using UK Measurements

Sarah Flower

ROBINSON

ROBINSON

First published in Great Britain in 2023
by Robinson

A CIP catalogue record for this book is available
from the British Library.

ISBN 978-1-47214-864-3

Designed by Thextension

Typeset in Madera
designed by Malou Verlomme for Monotype

Printed and bound in China

Papers used by Robinson are from well-
managed forests and other responsible sources.

Robinson
An imprint of Little, Brown Book Group
Carmelite House, 50 Victoria Embankment,
London EC4Y 0DZ

An Hachette UK Company
www.hachette.co.uk
www.littlebrown.co.uk

The recommendations given in this book are
solely intended as education and should not be
taken as medical advice.

The authorised representative
in the EEA is
Hachette Ireland
8 Castlecourt Centre
Dublin 15, D15 XTP3, Ireland
(email: info@hbgi.ie)

Contents

Chicken

Spicy Chicken Wings 78

Bacon-Wrapped Chicken with Mushroom & Cheese Stuffing 81

Sticky Chicken Drumsticks 82

Roast Chicken 85

Southern Fried Chicken 86

Thai-Style Chicken Skewers 89

Chicken Kiev 90

Chicken Ball Pittas 93

Asian-Inspired Chicken 94

Creamy Bacon & Thyme Chicken 97

Chicken Schnitzel 98

Tandoori-Style Chicken 101

Creamy Garlic & Spinach Stuffed Chicken 102

Meat

Toad in the Hole 107

Beef Lasagne 108

Roast Beef with Horseradish 111

Simple Gammon Joint 112

Pork Chops with Creamy Garlic Sauce 115

Chilli Con Carne 116

Warm Marinated Steak Salad 119

Lamb Burgers 120

Stuffed Loin of Pork 123

Crispy Pork Belly 124

Lamb Koftas 127

Fish & Seafood

Salmon, Potato & Chilli Fishcakes 131

Tuna & Sweetcorn Lasagne 132

Homemade Fish Fingers 135

Herby Cod 136

Loaded Salad Niçoise 139

Quick & Easy Garlic & Chilli Prawns 140

Butter & Herb Salmon Parcels 143

Vegan & Vegetarian

Baked Stuffed Aubergines 147

The Best Nut Roast 148

Spiced Tofu Burgers 151

Roasted Vegetable Salad with Feta 152

Garlic, Herb & Cherry Tomato Pasta Bake 155

Cauliflower & Broccoli Bake 156

Introduction

Welcome to my first air fryer book, *The Everyday Family Air Fryer Cookbook*. I do hope you enjoy using it. For those of you who don't already know, I am a nutritionist, recipe developer and author, and I have a passion for cooking.

As the title suggests, you will find a wide range of family-friendly air fryer recipes in this book. As a busy working mum, it is important to be able to create recipes that everyone enjoys, so you won't find any obscure ingredients in any of my books! But perhaps more importantly, with the rising costs of living, it is more crucial than ever that we are savvy in the kitchen. Far from being a gimmick, air fryers are actually a great tool to save you time and money, primarily because you don't have to waste energy heating and cooking in a large oven. Preheating is minimal (they heat up in seconds) and many models will cook your favourite dishes up to 30 per cent faster.

I have written lots of recipe books using a range of different kitchen gadgets; one such gadget was the halogen oven, which became very popular, and my books on this subject were bestsellers. They are very similar to air fryers, so if you have any halogen recipe books you will find that you can use their recipes with ease in the air fryer. I have also written several books on slow cookers as well as specialised diet books, so feel free to check them out too.

One thing I really want to stress: please read the technical chapters that follow, especially if you are new to the air fryer. They are fantastic machines but they do vary from brand to brand. As you can imagine, my kitchen is full of different gadgets; in fact, while writing this book, I used four different air fryers. You can find out more in Air Fryers: The Basics (see page 10) where I go into detail on the differences between air fryers and halogen ovens and which air fryers I use the most.

One of the biggest misconceptions about air fryers is that they are simply a healthy way to fry food. This doesn't really do them justice so I'd suggest you think of them instead as a fast-heating oven. This way you will add to your repertoire and use it to its full potential. Since I began using air fryers, I only use my main oven when cooking larger meals, such as a full roast dinner for the family, or when I want to bake large cakes.

I hope you enjoy the recipes and the delicious meals you are about to create as much as I have enjoyed creating them. If you do, maybe you would like to get in touch. It is always lovely to hear from readers. You can contact me by visiting my website at www.sarahflower.co.uk, on Twitter and Instagram @MsSarahFlower and on TikTok @SarahFlowerNutritionist. Feel free to tag me when sharing your food creations. I would love to see how you are getting on.

Sarah x

Air Fryers The Basics

The air fryer really is an incredibly versatile piece of kit, and we are even starting to see standard ovens manufactured with air fry options. Don't just think of your air fryer as a healthier way to fry food (as it was marketed initially and as the name suggests); think of it more as a versatile oven and this way you will open your mind to all sorts of possibilities.

Finding the right machine

There are so many machines on the market, it can be daunting to find the right one for you. Hopefully this book will help build your confidence to make this machine an integral part of your kitchen. No one wants to spend money on an expensive machine and then leave it to gather dust.

It is really important to think about how you are going to use your air fryer. Air fryers come in a variety of shapes and sizes, so if you have a family, you will probably be best considering a larger machine or dual machine, whereas if you are someone with limited space but like using kitchen gadgets, you may be better thinking about a multicooker, such as the Ninja Foodi. If you are someone who enjoys the ease of a conventional oven but likes the idea of an air fryer, you might want to look at a mini oven with air fryer options.

I am often asked what machine I use. There are so many great machines on the market, and I can't cover them all so if you are looking to buy a new machine, do your homework, read the reviews, check the warranty/guarantee offered and, as explained above, make sure you know what you want from your machine. While developing the recipes for this book, I used four different air fryers:

1 Cuisinart Mini Oven (with air fry function) – a brilliant machine that looks like, and has the advantage of being, a multi-oven with several settings for different uses. It is approximately the size of a microwave oven, with a pull-down door and two shelves. It has seven different cooking functions and heats up in 90 seconds. I use it all the time and love the fact I can use regular baking trays and ovenproof dishes in this. I find the air fryer less powerful than the Lakeland Dual Basket (see page 12), so things can sometimes take fractionally longer to cook, but it really is barely noticeable.

2 Ninja Foodi – if you have seen any of my slow cooker books, you will know I am a huge fan of the Ninja Foodi. This is a 9-in-1 machine that includes functions for air frying, pressure cooking, slow cooking, sauté, baking and more. This is a great machine, especially if you have limited space and don't want multiple gadgets in the kitchen. The old Foodi (which I have) had a separate lid for pressure cooking, but the new machines are much improved with just one hinged lid for all applications. From an air fryer point of view only, I do prefer the Cuisinart and the Lakeland Dual Basket, but as a multicooker, it is very hard to beat.

3 Lakeland Dual Basket Air Fryer – this is great for families who love air frying. As the name suggests, there are two air fry rectangle drawers, one large and one small, perfect for when you have a few things to cook for one meal. One side has a 5.5-litre capacity and the other 3.5 litres. It also has simple touch display and nine pre-sets to help you. I love Lakeland, but Ninja also has a similar machine. While I have not used the Ninja, I would still recommend it as their products are always great.

4 Lakeland Digital Crisp Air Fryer – this is a single-drawer air fryer, with a round drawer. This is one of the most popular designs for air fryers. It has eight pre-sets to help you when starting out. It does not take up as much space as the Lakeland Dual Basket and I can see the appeal of this size for people who live alone and couples, but also for those who may be nervous about using the machine. However, I do warn you: once you have the air frying bug, you may want to progress to a larger machine!

Halogen ovens versus air fryers

I have published several books on the halogen oven. I am often asked how they compare to air fryers so here are some of the key differences:

The technical bit An air fryer uses rapid air circulation technology to cook food, while a halogen oven uses a halogen bulb and a fan to cook food. So really, they are based on very similar principles, and you may find some recipes work well for both machines.

Size and cooking capacity Air fryers are generally smaller than halogen ovens and have a smaller cooking capacity, but it depends on the size of the machine you opt for and, as stated earlier in this chapter, machines do vary a lot. If you have a standard, single-drawer air fryer, the drawer will be smaller than the halogen oven, which means things like cake tins and ovenproof dishes may not fit, but there are ways around all of this.

Cooking time Air fryers use rapid air circulation technology, so speed can be a great asset, but it also depends on what you are cooking. The cooking time and temperature for air fryer recipes are usually different than those for standard oven recipes – air fryers cook at a higher temperature for shorter cooks. Cakes tend to be the exception to this rule. One of the big selling points of the halogen oven when it hit the market 10–15 years ago was the speed of cooking, however, when I released my halogen oven cookery books, I encouraged people to slow down the cooking speed and lower the temperature. People were so fixated on speed they ended up burning the outside of the food while not cooking it fully on the inside, leaving them with a raw centre. Thankfully this is not such an issue when cooking with an air fryer.

Cooking functions Air fryers are designed specifically for air frying but can also perform other cooking functions such as baking, grilling, steaming and roasting. On the other hand, halogen ovens are designed primarily for cooking food through convection and are more like mini ovens in that respect. It's always best to consult a recipe specifically designed for the air fryer, or to experiment with a standard oven recipe to find the optimal temperature and cooking time for your air fryer. Remember to check your food frequently and adjust the temperature and cooking time as needed to ensure it is cooked through and crispy on the outside.

Energy efficiency I personally don't think there is much difference, but having looked into this, it is thought the halogen bulb used in the oven consumes less energy compared to the motor and heating element used in the air fryer.

Pros and cons I loved my halogen oven, with the warm glow it emitted when lit up and the 360-degree view of the food as it cooked, but the glass bowl was heavy to wash. Some halogen ovens have hinged lids, which are better, but most have detachable lids for which you need a safe surface to set them down on when hot. The air fryer is practical for all the family and for cooking a surprisingly large number of meals. It has the advantage of being much cheaper to run than a standard oven and is perfect for those quick heats that most family meals require. The amount of cooking space can be an issue, so it is important to buy the right machine for your requirements. You can't see the food cooking, so you may need to open the drawers and check periodically if you are a newbie.

Having said all of the above, what is my overall verdict? Well, the fact that I no longer have a halogen oven probably speaks for itself!

Accessories

You can use your air fryer by cooking directly in the drawers or basket but just like conventional ovens, air fryers can also be used with ovenproof dishes and other accessories when cooking. This is great for things like cakes or wet recipes, and this makes the air fryer function more like a small oven as you are not using the circulating air to crisp the food.

Remember these machines get very hot and often there is limited space to get things in and out of the baskets, so be careful as you can easily burn yourself.

Most air fryers currently on the market don't come with any additional accessories. There are many extras you can buy, but some are better than others. Here is my list of accessories which I believe will make your air fryer much more versatile.

Silicone liners: These are great as they not only save on washing up, prevent sticking and help lift the food out with ease, but they also increase the usability of your air fryer. You can buy silicone liners specific to the size of your air fryer and – as with most things – quality can vary depending on the price you pay. I have purchased various sets online and I prefer a more structured silicone liner.

Paper liners: These are disposable liners, similar to large cake liners. They are relatively cheap and work well. They can help prevent the food sticking as well as help you lift out the food with ease.

Accessory kits: You can buy dedicated accessory kits but do make sure the measurements will fit your air fryer. These can include racks, cake tins, tongs, skewers, and silicone cupcake or muffin cases. As these are designed to fit into the air fryer, you will notice the cake tins will probably be much smaller than standard cake tins.

✱ *Cooking racks:* These help create layers in your air fryer. For example, if cooking a breakfast, you can pop your sausages on the base of the drawer to cook, then add a rack to pop the bacon on in the last 5–8 minutes of cooking.

✱ *Silicone tongs:* Always useful to remove food but also to help turn the food if required. Silicone is important as you do not want to scratch the air fryer lining.

✱ *Skewers:* Great to cook kebabs or any food that needs to be rotated during cooking.

✱ *Cake tins:* You may be surprised how small some of these can be. If you have a smaller machine, you may find you need to cook your food in batches or make smaller cakes to suit. I have a selection of tins and ovenproof dishes that fit in my air fryers, plus I use silicone cake cases and ramekin dishes in various sizes.

✱ *Silicone cupcake cases:* I love these and use mine all the time. I tend to line mine with paper cases as well, purely so the cakes have a paper case on them when cooked as it makes them easier to handle and store.

* *Pizza pan:* These tend to have non-stick coating and holes in to allow a full cook in the air fryer.

* *Toast rack:* Some accessory kits come with a small toast rack, so you can cook your toast vertically, and some of these have slots to hold eggs, perfect for soft- or hard-boiled eggs.

* *Silicone pan pads:* These are basically very small oven gloves to help you lift things out of your air fryer without burning your fingers.

* *Silicone mats:* These can be placed inside the air fryer and are great for cooking on without mess.

* *Silicone oil brush:* While the air fryer is known as an oil-free fryer, this refers to the fact you do not have to use oil to create crispy foods. However, we do use oil to coat some foods and a silicone brush or light spray of olive oil works brilliantly when a light coating is required.

* *Plate clamps:* These help you lift out the racks or pans. I must admit I rarely use these.

Meat thermometer: Highly recommended if you are cooking meat in your air fryer. Machines do vary and our recipes are a guide, so I do advise you to check your food periodically and adjust the cooking times accordingly.

Ovenproof dishes: You can use a variety of ovenproof dishes and bakeware in your air fryer, the key is ensuring they fit! I have a variety of small ovenproof dishes, some silicone cake cases and tin moulds, as well as ramekin dishes.

New machine smell

Some machines give off a not-so-pleasant smell when they are first used. I did not notice this at all with the Mini Oven or the Ninja Foodi, but really noticed it with the Dual Basket Air Fryer. I ended up placing it in the garage and set it for an hour to help burn off the smell. This can be very common for new machines and your instruction manual should mention this.

How to Use Your Air Fryer

If you are new to air frying, you may be a bit unsure when starting out. Here are my top tips to help ease you into the wonderful world of air frying.

Variations in machines

As you have read in the previous chapter, I actually have three machines, all very different in size, shape and design. The most common type has a drawer system, where I place food into the basket and slot the drawer back in. One has a hinged lid, allowing me to place items into the air fryer basket from above. My other air fryer is a mini oven with shelves. Get to know your machine as temperatures, timings and size all vary. For ease, in this book I refer to filling the air fryer 'basket' as this is the most common type of air fryer. I am also focusing on family size, so if you have a smaller air fryer or are cooking for one, you will need to adjust or cook in batches.

Read the manual

I know it is boring and something most of us prefer not to spend our time doing, but I highly recommend you read your machine's user manual. It will explain how it works, the different settings and safety precautions. It will tell you how to clean it before use (to avoid a horrible smell on the first cook), how to clean it after use and any essential dos and don'ts for your particular machine.

Cooking times

Please get to know your machine as cooking times can really vary between machines – for this reason the times stated in these recipes are for guidance and may need tweaking. If you are converting a conventional oven recipe to an air fryer, it is common for the timings to be approximately 20 per cent quicker and the temperature tends to be between 10°C and 20°C less. I always prefer to cook at a lower temperature for longer. Note that when your air fryer has reached the allotted time programmed in, it will turn off. This means you can rest easy that if the phone rings or you are called away from the kitchen, your food won't spoil.

There are many air fryer recipes online, but a huge number of these are aimed at the US market. Here is a basic table to help you convert oven temperatures from Fahrenheit to Celsius.

FAHRENHEIT	CELSIUS	FAHRENHEIT	CELSIUS
200°F	95°C	365°F	185°C
225°F	110°C	370°F	187°C
250°F	120°C	375°F	190°C
275°F	135°C	385°F	195°C
300°F	150°C	390°F	200°C
325°F	165°C	400°F	205°C
350°F	175°C	410°F	210°C
355°F	180°C		

Preheating

As with cooking in a conventional oven, it's always best to put your prepared food into a hot air fryer. Unlike conventional ovens, however, air fryers can get to temperature in as little as 30 seconds to 1 minute, although this will vary depending on the brand and size of your air fryer and some larger models may take up to 5 to 10 minutes. It's a good idea to get to know your machine so that you know when is the best time to switch your machine on – that way it will be ready to go when you are.

Basket

Depending on the type of air fryer you own, you may have a sliding drawer or basket. Some of these baskets come with a fixed shelf at the base (allowing a small area for air to circulate under this), and in some machines this is removable. The air fryer works by circulating heat, but you can cook with ovenproof dishes and silicone or paper liners. I have also cooked directly into the basket with this small shelf removed. Refer to your manufacturer's guidelines for more advice as all machines are different.

Ovenproof dishes

You may have to be creative if your air fryer is on the small side so I recommend investing in some small ovenproof dishes and ramekins. Ramekins are brilliant in the air fryer, and you can get them in different sizes. I have several small ones which are great for making your favourite desserts in individual portions. I also have some larger ones that work perfectly if you are cooking for two or three.

Depending on the size of your air fryer, an ovenproof dish can often be a challenge to remove from the basket when hot. I usually opt for a piece of foil, around 30–50cm long, ensuring there is enough to go around the dish and a little more so you can lift it out. Fold the foil lengthways until you have a strong strap about 5cm wide. Place the strap in the centre of your air fryer and place your ovenproof dish on top, ensuring there is enough foil either side to use as a strap when you need to lift out the dish. Fold or lay the excess over the top or sides of the dish during cooking. When you need to remove the dish, simply unfold the straps and lift it out of the basket.

Cake tins

There are various accessory packs you can buy online but do read the descriptions carefully – particularly the dimensions. I ordered a few to see the variety and some did make me laugh: some of the items were tiny! I had a loaf tin in miniature and muffin tins that are so small you would struggle to get a good mouthful. I use silicone cupcake moulds, which are brilliant, but do buy good-quality ones or they can be a bit floppy. I line these with traditional paper cases, which makes them easier to handle once cooked.

Liners

I love silicone liners as they can transform how you use your air fryer. They can prevent foods sticking, save on washing up and also work well with foods that are best cooked slightly wet, such as roasted vegetables or pasta sauces. You just wash them, and they can be used time and time again. You can buy them to fit your shape and make of air fryer.

Top tips for air frying

Start with simple recipes
As a beginner, start with simple recipes that are easy to prepare. You'll find a selection of quick and easy everyday suggestions on pages 22–25. These recipes will help you get familiar with the air fryer and how it cooks food.

Don't overcrowd the basket
Overcrowding the air fryer basket or drawer with too much food can prevent the hot air from circulating properly and lead to uneven cooking. It's better to cook in batches if needed.

Use cooking spray or oil sparingly
Air fryers require less oil than traditional frying methods, so use cooking spray or oil sparingly. A little goes a long way and can help to achieve a crispy exterior on your food.

Check the food frequently
If you are unsure of or new to a recipe or machine, I would strongly advise you to keep an eye on the food as it cooks. For example, if a recipe gives a cooking time of 20 minutes, I would suggest you check the food after 15 minutes to ensure that it doesn't burn or overcook.

Shake or flip the food

To ensure even cooking, shake or flip the food in the air fryer basket halfway through the cooking time. This is important for foods such as chips, sausages or similar.

Experiment with different recipes

Don't be afraid to experiment with different recipes and ingredients. Air fryers can be used for a wide range of foods, from appetisers to main dishes and desserts.

How to clean your air fryer

Refer to the manufacturer's guidelines as machines do vary. Always clean your air fryer after every use, making sure the air fryer is unplugged and has cooled down before cleaning. Remove the basket and tray and wash with warm, soapy water, using either a non-abrasive sponge or cloth to clean them. Make sure to rinse them well and dry them thoroughly.

Do not use abrasive materials that may scratch the surface of the air fryer. Air fryers have a non-stick coating which can scratch easily, so treat it with care in order to preserve this. Some of the components are dishwasher-safe, but I personally prefer to wash them by hand as I find dishwashers can start to destroy some non-stick coatings after frequent washing.

CONVERSION CHARTS

WEIGHT

Metric	Imperial
25g	1oz
50g	2oz
75g	3oz
100g	4oz
150g	5oz
175g	6oz
200g	7oz
225g	8oz
250g	9oz
300g	10oz
350g	12oz
400g	14oz
450g	1lb

LIQUIDS

Metric	Imperial	US cup
5ml	1 tsp	1 tsp
15ml	1 tbsp	1 tbsp
50ml	2fl oz	3 tbsp
60ml	2½fl oz	¼ cup
75ml	3fl oz	⅓ cup
100ml	4fl oz	scant ½ cup
125ml	4½fl oz	½ cup
150ml	5fl oz	⅔ cup
200ml	7fl oz	scant 1 cup
250ml	9fl oz	1 cup
300ml	½ pint	1¼ cups
350ml	12fl oz	1⅓ cups
400ml	¾ pint	1¾ cups
500ml	17fl oz	2 cups
600ml	1 pint	2½ cups

MEASUREMENTS

Metric	Imperial
5cm	2in
10cm	4in
13cm	5in
15cm	6in
18cm	7in
20cm	8in
25cm	10in
30cm	12in

SYMBOLS

Double up and freeze

Vegetarian

Vegan

Dairy-free option

Quick & Easy
Air Fryer Cooking

Here is my guide to some everyday items perfect for your air fryer.

Bacon	200°C	Place the bacon on a rack inside the air fryer to allow air to circulate; ensure the rashers do not overlap. Cook for 5–8 minutes, depending on thickness and desired crispiness.
Boiled egg	180°C	Place the egg in the air fryer, or you can use the egg trays that come with some accessory packs.
		Soft-boiled egg – 5–6 minutes
		Hard-boiled egg – 8–10 minutes
Poached egg	185°C	Pour boiling water (from a kettle) into your ramekin. Crack the egg into the boiling water, pop the ramekin into your air fryer basket and cook for 5–6 minutes. If you preheat the air fryer before cooking, you can reduce the cooking time by 30 seconds to 1 minute.
Crumpets	190°C	Cook for 3–4 minutes, then turn and cook for another 1–2 minutes.
Frozen chips	200°C	Cook for 15–18 minutes, shaking the basket once or twice during cooking. For extra crispiness, spray with a light coating of olive oil before placing into the air fryer.
Naan bread	180°C	Cook for 1–3 minutes until warm.
Frozen garlic bread	180°C	Cook for 5–7 minutes, depending on size and thickness.
Baked potato	200°C	Rub the potato with oil and lightly season with salt, then prick several times with a fork before placing in the air fryer basket. Cook for 40–60 minutes.

Frozen chicken nuggets, fish fingers (or similar)	190°C	Place into the air fryer basket, ensuring they do not overlap. Cook for 10–15 minutes, depending on the product. For extra crispiness, spray with a light coating of olive oil before placing into the air fryer.
Pastries	180°C	Place the pastry into the air fryer basket and cook for 5 minutes.
Roasted vegetables: carrots, courgette, aubergine, peppers, parsnips, cauliflower	180°C	Place the vegetables into your lined basket. Drizzle with olive oil and cook for 12–20 minutes, turning occasionally. Timings depend on the type and size of the vegetables used.
Chicken breast	190°C	Place the seasoned/oiled chicken in the air fryer and cook for 20–25 minutes, depending on the size of the chicken breast.
Sausages	190°C	Place the sausages into your air fryer basket and cook for 15–20 minutes, depending on size and thickness of the sausages. A lower temperature is more suited for chipolata sausages. Shake halfway through cooking to ensure they are browned evenly.
Toasted wraps	190°C	Place your chosen filling into the centre of each wrap and fold to form a parcel. Place in your air fryer basket and cook for 5–6 minutes until golden.

OPPOSITE

1 Crispy Bacon

2 Roasted Vegetables

3 Warming Naan Bread

4 Boiled Egg

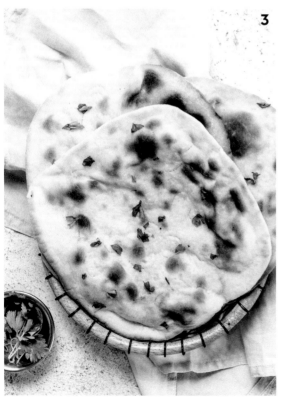

1

Breakfasts

Breakfast time during the week is always a rushed affair so it's important to remember that the air fryer is your friend and will save you time and money. Air fryers cook food faster than traditional ovens, which means you can prepare your breakfast in a fraction of the time. This can be particularly useful if you're in a rush in the morning and don't have a lot of time to spare. Plus, because air fryers are easy to clean, you won't have to spend a lot of time washing up after breakfast.

Whether it is a quick reheat or you are baking fresh croissants, right through to a full cooked breakfast with the crispiest bacon, the air fryer has your back. I also make my granola in the air fryer, which then gets stored in airtight jars. And don't forget to check out pages 23–24 for details on how to air fry some of your favourite breakfast items, from crispy bacon, boiled eggs and poached eggs to crumpets.

Chocolate Granola

Makes approx. 15 servings

300g mixed nuts (Brazil nuts, hazelnuts, almonds, macadamias, walnuts)

100g pecan nuts (these add a sweetness kids love)

75g flaked almonds

80g traditional rolled oats

100g unsweetened coconut flakes

75g sunflower seeds

75g pumpkin seeds

40g coconut oil

2 tbsp unsweetened cocoa or cacao powder

2 tbsp sugar or natural sweetener (or to taste)

NOTE

If you want added chocolate, you can stir in some chocolate chips (white, milk or dark), once cooled, or for a fruity kick, some dried raspberries and strawberries.

One for the kids or the chocoholics out there! It is really easy to make and there is nothing stopping you doubling or tripling the recipe to make up a large batch as it keeps well in a sealed, airtight container. I keep mine in a large glass jar. I also have this as a snack with yoghurt, as a topping for some desserts or even in a bowl to munch in front of my favourite film!

Place all the nuts in a sealable freezer bag and bash with a rolling pin until they are in smaller bite-size pieces. I prefer doing it this way as it takes out my frustrations but also because using a food processor risks overprocessing them and if you are not careful you can end up with nutty dust!

Place the crushed nuts into a bowl and add the oats, coconut flakes and seeds.

Melt the coconut oil (either in a jug in the microwave or in a small pan on the hob). Once melted, add the cocoa powder and sweetener, and combine well. Pour over the nut mix and stir well until the oil coats all the nuts.

Pour the mixture into the lined air fryer basket. I use a silicone liner, but you can use a paper liner or large piece of baking parchment. You may need to cook this in batches depending on the size of your air fryer. Spread the mixture out until it covers the base.

Set your air fryer to 170°C and bake for 3-4 minutes before turning the nuts and baking again for another 3-4 minutes. You can stir every couple of minutes if you wish, for a more even cook.

Remove the granola from the air fryer and allow to cool completely. Once cooled, store in an airtight container and keep in a dry, cool place for no more than 2 weeks. It can also be frozen.

Plain Omelette

Serves 1

2 large eggs

60ml milk

seasoning, to taste

Optional toppings

chopped ham

grated cheese

vegetables, such as diced red pepper, spinach, halved cherry tomatoes

You probably wouldn't think of making omelettes in an air fryer, but they actually work really well. This is a plain omelette recipe, but you can top or fill it with your chosen fillings. Great for breakfast or lunch, omelettes can be very versatile, and as they are packed full of protein, should keep you feeling fuller for longer.

In a bowl, whisk together the eggs and milk, and season well.

Line your air fryer basket. I use a silicone liner, but you can use paper liners if you prefer.

Pour the egg mixture into the lined air fryer basket.

Set your air fryer to 180°C and cook the omelette for 6–8 minutes, or until it is set, light and puffed up and cooked through. If you are adding any fillings, you can do this after 6 minutes: add to one side of the omelette and then flip one side over to cover the filling, before continuing to cook for the remaining few minutes.

Serve immediately.

Cheesy Garlic & Basil Tomatoes

Serves 2

3 tomatoes, halved

1-2 garlic cloves, roughly chopped

a few basil leaves, chopped, plus extra to garnish (optional)

black pepper, to taste

drizzle or spray of olive oil

50–75g Cheddar or red Leicester cheese, grated

These are absolutely delicious and perfect when served with scrambled egg. If you are vegan, you can omit the cheese and serve the tomatoes with some scrambled tofu.

Place the halved tomatoes, cut side up, in your lined air fryer basket.

Place the garlic and basil on top of each of the tomato halves. Season with black pepper and finish with a drizzle or spray of olive oil.

Set your air fryer to 180°C and cook for 6 minutes until they have started to soften. Add the cheese and cook for another 2–3 minutes.

Garnish with more basil leaves (if using) and serve with scrambled egg, scrambled tofu, or crispy bacon with slices of avocado.

Easy Fresh Baked Croissants

Makes 6

1 x 350g pack of croissant dough (I use Jus-Rol)

1 egg, beaten

NOTE

These are great when stuffed with sweet or savoury fillings. You can also reheat them in the air fryer for a few minutes.

It is always lovely to start the day with fresh pastries. Here I've used ready-made croissant dough, but if you are adventurous, you can of course make your own croissant dough from scratch. If you don't want to bake and eat all six croissants you can freeze the unbaked rolled croissants for another time. To cook from frozen, I recommend reducing the temperature to 170°C and cooking for 10–12 minutes until golden.

Unroll the dough and lay it out before cutting into triangles. This is quite straightforward as the dough already has perforated lines for you to follow. You can use a knife or pizza cutter to do this.

Roll each triangle up to form a crescent and then brush with the beaten egg.

Line the air fryer basket with baking parchment or liner. Place the croissants into the basket, making sure they don't overlap (you may need to cook them in batches).

Set your air fryer to 180°C and bake for 8–10 minutes, until golden.

Baked Avocado Boats

Serves 1

1 avocado

2 eggs

50g diced pancetta
(or use bacon)

seasoning, to taste

1 spring onion, finely chopped

I love this breakfast, it's so easy and so filling. Here I've included some pancetta, spring onions and egg, but there are so many options. I sometimes add a pinch of chilli flakes, or a sprinkle of grated cheese. Feel free to experiment!

Cut the avocado in half, removing the stone.

Making sure your avocado halves sit level, crack your eggs into the gap left by the stone.

Sprinkle the pancetta over the egg and season to taste.

Set your air fryer to 190°C, place the boats into your air fryer basket and bake for 10 minutes.

Scatter over the spring onion before serving.

Soft-Boiled Eggs with Avocado & Bacon Soldiers

Serves 2

2 avocados

6 rashers of streaky smoked bacon, cut in half

2 soft-boiled eggs
(see Note)

NOTE

To cook the eggs in the air fryer

Place the eggs in the air fryer basket and turn on to 120°C. Cook for 8–10 minutes, depending on how you like them done.

To cook the eggs on the hob

Place the eggs into a saucepan of boiling water and cook for 4–6 minutes, depending on how you like them done.

This is my take on that classic childhood favourite of soft-boiled egg and soldiers. It is really lovely. If you have a dual basket air fryer, you could cook both the eggs and the avocado and bacon soldiers in the same air fryer. If not, just cook your soft-boiled eggs in the traditional way. Remember, eggs should be at room temperature before you cook them.

Cut each avocado in half and remove the stone. Carefully remove the skin – I use a spoon for this – and scoop out the flesh in one piece. Chop each half into 3 wedges, so you end up with 12 wedges in total.

Wrap each wedge in a strip of streaky bacon.

Set your air fryer to 180°C, place the wedges into your air fryer basket and cook for 6–8 minutes until the bacon is crispy.

Remove from the air fryer and serve with your freshly cooked, soft-boiled eggs.

Mini Frittata Muffins

Makes 6

4 eggs, beaten

1 tbsp butter, melted

150ml milk

1 tsp dried oregano or mixed herbs

6 tbsp finely chopped vegetables of your choice

60g grated or crumbled cheese of your choice

seasoning, to taste

So easy and great for a breakfast or packed lunch. You can even prep these the night before, ready to pop into the oven in the morning. I add whatever vegetables need using up in my fridge – peppers, spring onions, courgette, tomatoes or spinach. You can also use any leftover cooked vegetables.

Place the eggs in a jug with the melted butter, milk, herbs and seasoning.

Line six silicone cupcake cases with paper cupcake liners.

Place a tablespoon of finely chopped vegetables into each muffin case and then divide the grated cheese evenly among them.

Pour over the egg mixture until they are two-thirds full.

Set your air fryer to 175°C and bake for 20 minutes until golden. They will rise but sadly drop again once cooled. Don't worry, they still taste divine!

Serve hot or cold. These also freeze well and can be reheated in the air fryer.

Vanilla & Blueberry Omelette

Serves 1

2 large eggs

60ml milk

1 tsp sugar

1 tsp vanilla bean paste

½ tsp ground cinnamon
(optional)

handful of blueberries

crème fraîche or Greek
yoghurt, to serve

I love a sweet omelette, especially when served with a dollop of crème fraîche or Greek yoghurt. I have used blueberries for this recipe, but you can use raspberries or blackberries too. Frozen berries can work but they can make the omelette quite wet.

In a bowl, whisk together the eggs, milk, sugar, vanilla and cinnamon (if using).

Line your air fryer basket. I use a silicone liner, but you can use paper liners if you prefer.

Pour the egg mixture into the lined air fryer basket.

Set your air fryer to 180°C and cook the omelette for 6–8 minutes, or until it is set, puffed up (light and fluffy) and cooked through.

Remove from the air fryer and flip the omelette onto your plate (the browner side will now be on the bottom). Place the blueberries on one side and flip the other side over to cover the berries.

Serve immediately with a dollop of crème fraîche or Greek yoghurt.

Crushed Avocado & Poached Egg on Sourdough Toast

Serves 2

2–4 fresh eggs

2–4 slices of sourdough bread

1 ripe avocado

butter, for spreading

chilli flakes (optional)

seasoning, to taste

Avocado and egg is really the most amazing combination, but it can be made even nicer if you add a rasher of bacon to it! I like to mash my avocado and season it well with salt and pepper and a sprinkle of chilli flakes, but you can use slices of avocado if you prefer. Fresh eggs are always best for the perfect poached eggs.

Boil the kettle to ensure you have just-boiled water for the eggs.

Once the hot water has boiled, fill two ramekins with water to about two-thirds full, then crack an egg into each one.

Set your air fryer to 175°C, place the ramekins in the air fryer basket and cook for 5–6 minutes.

Meanwhile toast your bread. While it is toasting, crush the avocado and season well to taste.

Butter the toast and then spread with the avocado. Sprinkle with chilli flakes (if using).

Remove the eggs from the air fryer, drain off the water and add a poached egg on top of the avocado toast.

Season the egg to taste and serve immediately.

French Toast

Serves 2

2 eggs

160ml whole milk

1 tsp vanilla bean paste

½ tsp ground cinnamon

4 slices of bread, cut in half

berries, crème fraîche and seeds, to serve

Who doesn't like French toast? This is so easy and you can also freeze the coated bread ready to toast, so why not make up some batches and freeze for another day? Kids love to make this but be warned: it can get messy. You can serve it with butter, jam or maple syrup, but I prefer mine with some fresh berries and crème fraîche.

Mix all the ingredients (apart from the bread) in a bowl until thoroughly combined. I prefer to do this in a large, shallow bowl as it can get messy.

Soak the bread slices in the mixture. Ensure you give the soaked bread slices a good shake before you place them in the air fryer basket, making sure they do not overlap. You may have to do this in batches.

Set your air fryer to 175°C and cook for 2 minutes before turning the bread over and cooking for another 2–3 minutes.

Serve immediately with berries, crème fraîche and seeds.

2

Lunches & Light Meals

Air fryers are not just for family meals, they are really useful for quick lunches, reheating and more. This can save you money as you don't have to turn the oven on to make your favourite quick and easy meals, snacks or ready meals. Pastries reheated in the air fryer remain crisp and delicious as if they had just come out of the oven – no more soggy pastry after a burst in the microwave! They are also brilliant for toasted sandwiches and wraps, and take just minutes, creating all-round crispness without the mess.

This chapter contains some of my favourite lunch suggestions.

Thai-style Bean Cakes

Serves 4

½ bunch of spring onions, roughly chopped

2 x 400g tins cannellini beans, drained and rinsed

handful of coriander leaves, finely chopped

1–2 tbsp red Thai curry paste

zest of 1 lime and the juice of ½

flour, for dusting

1 tsp olive oil, for brushing the cakes

These are great for a working lunch served with a delicious salad and some sweet chilli sauce to dip into. If you don't have cannellini beans, you can use chickpeas. These cakes can be stored in the fridge after cooking for 2–3 days or can be frozen.

Place the spring onions, beans, coriander, Thai curry paste and lime zest and juice in a food processor and pulse until combined – don't overprocess as you don't want the mixture too smooth.

Place the mixture on a floured board and form into 4 cakes/patties.

Brush the cakes with olive oil and place into the air fryer, making sure they don't overlap. Set your air fryer to 190°C and cook for 8 minutes, then turn them over and cook for another 4–6 minutes.

Serve with a sweet chilli sauce and salad leaves.

Mini Quiche Lorraine

Makes 4–6 small tartlets

For the pastry

150g plain flour, plus extra
for dusting

75g cold butter, diced

6 tbsp cold water

For the filling

300ml double cream

4 medium eggs

½ tsp mustard powder

150g Gruyère cheese, grated
(or use mature Cheddar)

1 small onion, finely chopped

200g diced lardons, pancetta
or smoky bacon

seasoning, to taste

Perfect for lunches, picnics or a light evening meal. This is a traditional quiche Lorraine, but you can change the fillings to suit. This recipe creates enough pastry and filling for 4–6 small tartlets, depending on the size of your tart tins. I have made my own pastry from scratch here, but you can of course use ready-made shortcrust pastry. If your air fryer basket is too small to fit all the tart tins at once, simply make this in two batches.

Put the flour into a large bowl and add small pieces of the chilled butter. Using your fingertips, rub the butter into the flour until the whole mix resembles breadcrumbs. Add 5–6 tablespoons of cold water, a little at a time, and mix until it forms a dough (you may not need all the water). Wrap the dough in cling film and place in the fridge to rest for 15 minutes.

Roll out the pastry on a floured surface to a thickness of about 3mm. Cut out circles to the correct size to line your tart tins and then press them into the tins.

Set your air fryer to 180°C, place the tarts inside and bake for 5 minutes until the pastry starts to colour slightly. You may have to do this in batches depending on the size of your air fryer.

Meanwhile, whisk the cream and eggs together, then stir in the remaining ingredients. Season well before pouring into the tartlets.

Place back into the air fryer and cook at 180°C for 15 minutes until the pastry is golden and the filling is just firm to the touch. These timings will depend on size and depth of the tins used so do check after 10 minutes.

Remove the tartlets from the air fryer and leave to cool before serving.

Scotch Eggs

Makes 4

5 medium eggs, at room temperature

400g good-quality gluten-free sausage meat

1 tsp dried thyme

1 tsp dried parsley

1 tsp dried sage

200g homemade breadcrumbs or crushed pork scratchings

50g Parmesan cheese, grated (optional)

2 tsp paprika

seasoning, to taste

You can substitute the dried herbs for finely chopped fresh herbs, if you have them, but you'll probably need to double the quantity to get the same flavour.

These are so worth the time it takes to make them as they really are far nicer than shop-bought scotch eggs. I prefer to use good-quality gluten-free sausage meat as it has far fewer nasties and a higher ratio of meat content.

Boil the kettle. Place 4 of the eggs in a saucepan, pour over the boiling water and place over a medium heat. Boil for 6 minutes. (You can also cook these in the air fryer if you prefer, see page 23.)

When the time is up, remove from heat and immediately drain away the hot water. Run the eggs under cold water, before leaving in the pan filled with cold water.

While they are cooling, place the sausage meat in a bowl, add the herbs and season well with salt and black pepper.

Peel the eggs, discarding the shells.

Divide the sausage meat into four and form each piece into a ball. Flatten each ball as much as you can. Place the egg in the centre and wrap the meat around the egg firmly until it is completely covered, pinching together to seal.

Break the remaining egg into a bowl and beat well. Place the breadcrumbs (or crushed pork scratchings), grated Parmesan (if using) and the paprika in another bowl, season and combine well. This is where it can get messy!

Dip each of the scotch eggs into the beaten egg, then in the breading mixture, turning to coat all sides evenly.

Set your air fryer to 190°C. Place the scotch eggs into the basket, making sure they don't touch each other. Cook for 15–20 minutes, shaking the basket occasionally during cooking to ensure a more even cook. They should be nice and golden.

Serve immediately or leave to cool before placing in an airtight container. Store in the fridge for up to 3 to 4 days.

Roasted Beetroot Falafels

Serves 4

2 beetroots, trimmed and
cut into bite-size chunks

1 tbsp olive oil

1 tbsp balsamic vinegar

2 x 400g tins chickpeas,
drained and rinsed

3–4 garlic cloves, crushed

1 small red onion, quartered

2 tbsp tahini, plus extra
to serve

1–2 tsp ground cumin

1 tsp ground coriander

½–1 tsp chilli powder

squeeze of lemon juice

seasoning, to taste

green salad leaves, to serve

**I love these falafels! The colour is amazing, and just
screams healthy. They are so easy to make and taste
delicious with a lovely selection of salad leaves – perfect
alfresco food. Thanks to the chickpeas, these falafels are
high in manganese, which is good for bone and joint
health, cognitive function and can help lower blood
sugar.**

Place the beetroot into the air fryer basket, spreading out
evenly, before drizzling with the olive oil and balsamic vinegar.
Season to taste.

Set your air fryer to 180°C and cook for 15–20 minutes until
roasted. Toss them regularly throughout the cooking time.

Place the cooked beetroot into a food processor along with
all the remaining ingredients and whizz to a moist paste.

Form into 8–10 balls or flat patties.

Place into the air fryer and cook at 190°C for 10–12 minutes,
tossing them regularly so they cook evenly.

Serve on a bed of green leaves and drizzle with some tahini.

The Everyday Family Air Fryer Cookbook

Quesadillas

Serves 2

2 tortilla wraps

75g cooked chicken, shredded

1 red or green pepper, deseeded and finely diced

2 spring onions, finely diced

2 tbsp Mexican spice paste or hot salsa sauce

75g Cheddar cheese, grated

seasoning, to taste

If you are using an air fryer with a basket you might want to try the parcel method – a simple, less messy option. Place the filling into the centre of one smaller wrap, ensuring you don't overload it. Fold in both sides and then roll up to enclose the filling in a parcel. Place in the air fryer basket with the seam down.

We all love a wrap. This recipe is for chicken quesadillas, so is great for using up any leftover chicken you may have in the fridge from the night before. These work equally well with leftover chilli, fajita filling or even just ham and cheese for a classic cheese and ham toastie wrap. Anything goes, so get creative.

Place one of the wraps on a chopping board. Add the chicken, pepper and onions and spread out evenly.

Drizzle over the paste or hot sauce before topping with the grated cheese. Add salt and pepper to taste.

Place the remaining wrap on top and press down gently. Depending on the size of your wraps and your basket, you may have to cut the wrap in half or into wedges to fit into your air fryer. This can be messy so you may prefer to follow the parcel method mentioned below.

Set your air fryer to 190°C and carefully place these into the air fryer basket. Cook for 5–7 minutes or until golden and heated through. Serve immediately.

Croque Monsieur

Serves 2

2 tbsp butter

1 tbsp plain flour

125ml milk

½ tsp Dijon mustard

4 slices of bread
(I use sourdough)

2 slices of ham

150g Cheddar cheese, grated
(or use Gruyère or a mixture
of both)

seasoning, to taste

This is my son's favourite. When he was little, he always opted for this in cafés for a quick lunch. It just seems much nicer than a standard toasted sandwich. Don't be afraid of making the béchamel sauce, it really is simple as long as you stay with it and stir.

In a small saucepan, melt the butter over a low-medium heat. Add the flour and whisk with a balloon whisk until it is nice and smooth. Gradually add the milk, whisking constantly, until the sauce thickens.

Add the Dijon mustard, season with salt and pepper, and whisk to combine. Remove from the heat.

Place 2 of the slices of bread on a board and spread some of the sauce on each slice.

Place a slice of ham and about a quarter of the grated cheese on top of each béchamel-topped sliced of bread, then top with the remaining slices of bread. Top each sandwich with the remaining béchamel and grated cheese.

Set your air fryer to 180°C. Place the sandwiches in the air fryer basket and cook for 5–7 minutes, or until the bread is crispy and the cheese is melted.

Serve hot and enjoy!

Baked Camembert

Serves 2-4

1 Camembert cheese

2 garlic cloves, finely chopped

1 sprig of fresh rosemary, leaves picked

1 tbsp olive oil

1 tbsp runny honey

seasoning, to taste

Baked Camembert is a delicious and easy lunch or appetiser that you can make in an air fryer. I have this with bread, toast or crackers - such great results with so little effort!

Remove the Camembert cheese from its packaging and place it in a small oven-safe dish or ramekin.

Use a sharp knife to score the top of the cheese in a crosshatch pattern.

Sprinkle the chopped garlic and rosemary over the top of the cheese, then drizzle over the olive oil and honey. Season with salt and pepper to taste.

Set your air fryer to 180°C. Place the dish or ramekin in the air fryer basket and cook for 5-7 minutes, or until the cheese is melted and bubbly.

Serve immediately with bread or crackers for dipping.

Roasted Tomato Soup

Serves 4

6 large tomatoes, quartered

1 large red onion, quartered

2–3 garlic cloves

1 red pepper, quartered and deseeded

1 carrot, cut into batons

1–2 sprigs of thyme

2 tbsp olive oil

1–2 tbsp balsamic vinegar

450ml vegetable stock

3 tbsp sundried tomato paste

250g tub of mascarpone

seasoning, to taste

I first made this soup when I was working with some schoolchildren and we were developing menus for an event. It was a massive hit and has become a firm favourite with all the family. The air fryer saves you from having to roast the vegetables in an oven, but the rest of the soup is done on the hob as air fryers and soups are not really compatible.

Put the tomatoes, onion, garlic, red pepper and carrot into a silicone liner or an ovenproof dish that will fit into your air fryer.

Place the sprigs of thyme in between the vegetables, then mix the olive oil and balsamic vinegar together and sprinkle over the vegetables. Season with salt and pepper.

Set your air fryer to 180°C and cook the vegetables for 15 minutes.

Remove the tomatoes and vegetables from the air fryer and place everything, including any juice, into a saucepan.

Add the stock and sundried tomato paste and use an electric hand blender (stick blender) to liquidise until smooth. If you prefer a smoother soup, you can pass it through a sieve.

Place over a medium heat on the hob and slowly warm it through. Add the mascarpone and continue to heat and stir for another 3–5 minutes before serving.

Cheese Soufflés

Serves 4

50g unsalted butter, plus
extra for greasing

30g plain flour

250ml whole milk

½ tsp salt

¼ tsp cayenne pepper

4 large eggs, separated

130g Gruyère cheese, grated

40g Parmesan cheese,
finely grated

chopped fresh herbs,
to garnish (optional)

These are delicious for a quick lunch or as a starter for a dinner party. Serve them as soon as they are ready, as soufflés do deflate after a few minutes when they start to cool.

In a saucepan, melt the butter over a low-medium heat. Add the flour and whisk using a balloon whisk until smooth.

Gradually add the milk, whisking constantly, until the mixture is smooth, thick and lump-free.

Add the salt and cayenne pepper and whisk to combine.

Remove the pan from the heat. Whisk in the egg yolks, one at a time, until well combined, stirring well between each egg yolk.

Stir in the grated Gruyère and Parmesan until melted and set aside to cool.

In a large clean bowl, beat the egg whites with an electric mixer until they form stiff peaks.

Place 1 spoonful of the egg white into the cheese mixture – this helps slacken the cheese mixture so that it's ready to combine fully.

Gently fold the remaining egg whites into the cheese mixture until just combined. Do this very slowly and carefully as you don't want to knock out the air from the egg whites.

Grease 4 ramekins with butter and divide the mixture evenly among them.

Set your air fryer to 185°C. Place the ramekins in the air fryer basket, leaving a little room in between for the air to circulate, and cook for 10–14 minutes until the soufflés are puffed up and golden brown.

Serve immediately, garnished with chopped herbs, if liked.

Courgette Pizza Bites

Serves 2-4

1–2 courgettes, thickly sliced into rounds

½ jar of sundried tomato paste

75-100g grated Cheddar cheese

50g pepperoni slices

These are so lovely and help you get some extra vegetables into your children without them realising. Ensure you cut the courgette into thick slices; too thin and they won't hold well. You can choose any topping, but in this recipe I am using sundried tomato paste, cheese and pepperoni.

Spread one side of the courgette rounds with the sundried tomato paste. Cover with cheese and your pepperoni. Repeat until all of the courgette rounds are covered.

Set your air fryer to 185°C. Place the bites into the basket, ensuring they are not overlapping, and cook for 5-7 minutes, or until the cheese is melted and bubbling well.

Serve immediately.

Crustless Spinach, Cheese & Bacon Quiche

Makes 8 slices

4 rashers of smoked bacon, diced

1 bunch of spring onions, finely chopped

50g mushrooms, sliced

50g baby leaf spinach

5 cherry tomatoes, quartered

120g mature Cheddar cheese, grated

6 medium eggs, beaten

200ml double cream

1 tsp dried oregano

1 tsp dried parsley

seasoning, to taste

I began making crustless quiches when I was first starting with a low-carb, grain-free way of eating and found I preferred them. I certainly didn't miss the pastry. Here is one of my favourites, packed with mushrooms, tomato, cheese, bacon and spinach. I have used rashers of bacon here, but you can use pancetta or lardons if you prefer.

Place the bacon pieces in the base of a silicone liner (while in the basket so you don't have to keep lifting it in and out) or, if you prefer, in an ovenproof dish. Top with all the vegetables and the cheese.

Mix the eggs and cream together in a jug until well combined. Add the herbs and season well.

Pour into the silicone liner or ovenproof dish until everything is covered.

Place in the air fryer and cook at 180°C for 25–35 minutes until it has risen, has a nice golden top and the middle is cooked.

Remove from the air fryer and serve either hot or cold.

Spicy Chicken Balls

Serves 4-6

500g chicken mince

1 small onion, finely chopped

2 garlic cloves

1 fresh chilli, finely chopped

½ tsp dried mint

½–1 tsp chilli powder

½ tsp ground cumin

1 tsp ground coriander

1 heaped tbsp almond butter

1 tbsp olive oil

These are a lighter version of a meatball, high in protein, low in fat and absolutely delicious. I love these served with salad or they can be stuffed into pitta breads. You can even use these for your spaghetti and meatball dish, though you may want to change the spices to traditionally Italian herbs for this.

These can be prepared a few hours in advance and placed in the refrigerator until ready.

Place all the ingredients in a bowl and combine well.

Use your hands to form into balls and place these onto a plate. Refrigerate until you are ready to cook.

Set your air fryer to 180°C.

Remove the chicken balls from the fridge and give them a light spray or drizzle with some olive oil, then place into the basket of your air fryer. Cook for 10–12 minutes, or until cooked through, shaking occasionally during cooking to ensure a more even cook.

Remove and serve with salad or stuffed into pitta. These are also great as a side dish with a curry.

3

Chicken

Chicken is one of the most popular meats in the UK and for good reason. It is packed with protein and is enjoyed by people of all ages. Most families opt for chicken breast, but for enhanced flavour I would recommend using thighs and leg meat, both of which have the added bonus that they are often much cheaper to buy.

If you are roasting a chicken for a Sunday lunch, buy a size bigger than you think you need and use the leftover meat (from all over the chicken, not just the breast and legs) to make yourself a chicken pie, chicken crumble, chicken fajitas or enchiladas, or even a curry. Don't forget to save the bones. They make an excellent and very nourishing chicken stock.

How to butterfly a chicken breast for stuffing or rolling

Place your hand over the breast and, using a very sharp knife, carefully cut through the breast horizontally, starting at the thickest edge and working your way to the thinnest, being careful not to cut through completely - you want the chicken breast to fold open like the wings of a butterfly or pages of a book. You must stop before you reach the edge. You can then open the chicken breast.

Cover with cling film and use a wooden kitchen mallet or rolling pin to bash lightly until you have a flat butterfly shape of chicken. This makes it much easier if you want to stuff and roll the chicken.

Once stuffed and rolled, you can hold it together with a wooden cocktail stick.

How to create a chicken pocket

Another option if you want to stuff a chicken breast is to create a pocket. This is useful if you want to stuff it with a few slices of mozzarella or similar.

Use a very sharp knife and cut into the thickest part of the chicken breast, making a cut about 4–5cm long to create a pocket – make sure you do not cut all the way through.

Once you have stuffed the chicken you can hold it together with a wooden cocktail stick to stop the stuffing coming out.

Spicy Chicken Wings

Serves 4

1 tbsp olive oil

2 heaped tsp paprika

2 tsp chilli powder

2 tsp garlic powder

2 tsp onion powder

1 tsp cayenne pepper

500g chicken wings, patted dry

sprinkle of sesame seeds

seasoning, to taste

fresh parsley, chopped, to garnish

sweet chilli sauce, to serve

NOTE

The cooking time may vary depending on the size and brand of your air fryer. Keep an eye on the wings and adjust the cooking time as needed.

Chicken wings are often underrated. They are cheap to buy and make a delicious meal. If you are nervous about cooking chicken wings or not a fan of them, you could use this recipe on chicken thighs or breast, but do adjust the timings to suit.

In a large bowl, mix together the olive oil, paprika, chili powder, garlic powder, onion powder and cayenne pepper, then add some salt and pepper.

Add the chicken wings to the bowl and toss to coat the wings evenly.

Place the wings in the air fryer basket in a single layer, leaving a little space between each wing, ensuring they don't overlap. You may need to cook these in batches depending on the size of your air fryer.

Set your air fryer to 190°C and cook the wings for 10 minutes, then flip them over and cook for another 10 minutes.

Check to make sure the wings are cooked through and crispy. If they are not fully cooked, cook them for an additional 2–3 minutes.

Sprinkle with sesame seeds. Serve the wings hot with sweet chilli sauce for dipping.

Bacon-Wrapped Chicken with Mushroom & Cheese Stuffing

Serves 4

4 skinless chicken breasts (approx. 600g)

150g mature Cheddar cheese, grated

80g chestnut mushrooms, sliced

2 garlic cloves, crushed

small handful of fresh basil, chopped

seasoning, to taste

200g back or streaky smoked bacon

green steamed vegetables, to serve

This is one of the most perfect flavour combinations and to me is the ultimate comfort dish: cheese, chicken, bacon and mushrooms, what's not to like? You can prepare these in advance and store in the fridge until you are ready to add to the air fryer.

Butterfly the chicken breast using a very sharp knife (see page 77). Start at the thickest edge and work to the thinnest, being careful not to cut through – you want the chicken to fold open like the wings of a butterfly. If it is uneven, just bash a little with a wooden rolling pin until it forms a flat butterfly ready for you to stuff and roll.

Place a generous layer of cheese, mushrooms, garlic and basil in the middle of the chicken breasts and season. Carefully roll the chicken breast to form a cylinder. Cover the chicken with your bacon, using this to help wrap and secure it. You can secure them with a wooden cocktail stick if you prefer, otherwise place them seam down into the air fryer basket.

Set your air fryer to 180°C and cook for 25–30 minutes.

Serve on a bed of green steamed vegetables.

Sticky Chicken Drumsticks

Serves 4

4–6 chicken drumsticks

2 tbsp runny clear honey

2 tbsp Worcestershire sauce

2 tbsp tomato ketchup

1 tbsp paprika

1 chilli, deseeded and finely chopped

1 tsp chilli powder

½ tsp cayenne pepper

seasoning, to taste

These are so simple to make and taste amazing. They can be served as a main meal with some rice and salad, or you can serve them cold for a lovely, packed lunch or picnic.

Score the thickest part of the chicken drumsticks a few times with a sharp knife.

Combine the remaining ingredients in a bowl, then use a pastry brush to brush this mixture onto each of the drumsticks, ensuring they are evenly coated.

Place the drumsticks into your air fryer basket. You can line the basket if you prefer less mess to wash up (it can get sticky), but they do crisp better when placed directly into the basket.

Set your air fryer to 190°C and cook for 20 minutes, turning during cooking to ensure an even cook. Check the chicken is cooked through before serving as timings can vary depending on machine and size of the chicken drumstick.

Serve hot or cold.

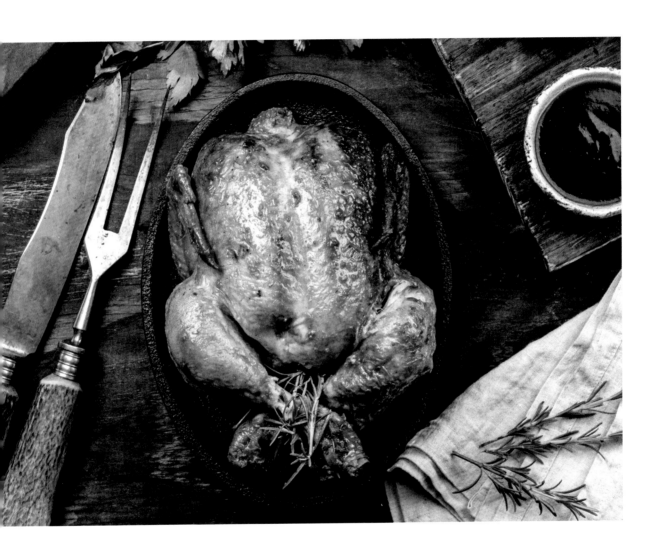

The Everyday Family Air Fryer Cookbook

Roast Chicken

Serves 4

1 medium-sized chicken (approx. 1.2kg)

1 red onion

1 lemon

30g butter

1–2 tsp fresh thyme or rosemary

seasoning, to taste

NOTE

Timings are approximate. The cooking temperature of your machine and size of your chicken can cause differences in cooking time. To check the chicken is cooked, ensure the juices run clear. You can also check the temperature of the chicken with a meat thermometer, which should read at least 75°C when pushed into the thickest part of the chicken, usually the thigh.

Yes, you can cook a whole roast chicken in your air fryer, but obviously it depends on the size of your air fryer. It does need to be big enough to comfortably fit the chicken into the basket – or the shelf if you have the mini oven. I cook mine breast side down for the first 50 minutes as I find it creates a juicer chicken when cooked this way, but that is entirely optional.

Prepare your chicken according to your own preference. I place 1 red onion and 1 lemon, both cut in half, into the cavity of the bird to enhance the flavour. I then rub the skin with butter and sprinkle with thyme or rosemary. You can also push herb butter under the skin. Season to taste.

Place the chicken, breast side down, into your air fryer basket.

Set your air fryer to 185°C and cook for 50 minutes, then turn the chicken over and cook for a further 20–30 minutes.

Serve with roast potatoes (see page 174) and steamed vegetables.

Southern Fried Chicken

Serves 4-6

1 large egg, beaten

500g skinless chicken pieces (can be drumstick, thigh or breast)

For the spice mix

150g plain flour (you can also use semolina or coconut flour)

4 tsp paprika

1 tsp dried parsley

3 tsp chicken seasoning (make sure this is sugar-free)

1 tsp dried oregano

½ tsp dried tarragon

1 tsp dried thyme

1 tsp garlic powder

½ tsp onion powder

½ tsp celery salt

generous seasoning of black pepper

If you love southern fried chicken, you must try this recipe. This is a healthy version your family will love. I recommend mixing a large batch of the herbs and spices and placing them in a jar so it is to hand whenever you want to make this - believe me, it will soon become a firm favourite.

Mix all the ingredients for the spice mix together in a large bowl, making sure the herbs and spices are evenly distributed into the flour.

Place the beaten egg in a dish.

Now for the messy bit — dip the chicken into the egg, then into the spice mixture, ensuring it is evenly covered. If you prefer, you can place the spiced flour mixture into a large bag, add the egg-coated chicken to the bag and shake well until evenly covered.

Carefully place the chicken into your air fryer basket, ensuring they are evenly spaced and not overlapping. They can be cooked in batches if there isn't enough room in your air fryer.

Set your air fryer to 190°C and cook for 20-25 minutes depending on the size of your chicken pieces.

Thai-style Chicken Skewers

Serves 4

300g chicken breast, diced (approx. 2 chicken breasts)

2 garlic cloves, crushed

2cm piece of fresh ginger, grated

1 chilli, deseeded and finely chopped

zest of 1 lime

4 tbsp coconut cream or Greek yoghurt

small handful of fresh coriander, finely chopped

seasoning, to taste

These are great served on a bed of rice. They can be made and cooked immediately but they are better if you have time to marinate them for at least 2 hours – or even overnight – before you make them.

If you are using wooden skewers, soak them well before using. You can also use metal skewers but make sure they will fit into your air fryer.

Cut the chicken into bite-size chunks. Place these into a bowl or Ziplock freezer bag.

Add all the remaining ingredients and season to taste. Combine well and leave to marinate.

When you are ready to cook, thread the chicken onto the pre-soaked skewers. You may need to cut the skewers to size (if they are wooden) in order to fit them in the air fryer.

Set your air fryer to 185°C, then place the skewers into the air fryer basket. Cook for 15–20 minutes, turning them halfway through to ensure an even cook.

Serve on a bed of rice or with some chilli dipping sauce.

Chicken Kiev

Serves 4

100g plain flour

2 eggs

150g breadcrumbs

50g freshly grated Parmesan (optional)

2 tsp dried parsley

2 tsp dried oregano

1 tsp paprika

1 tsp onion granules

4 skinless chicken breasts (approx. 400g)

seasoning, to taste

For the garlic butter

3-4 garlic cloves, crushed or chopped

150g butter, softened

small handful of parsley, finely chopped

zest of ½ lemon

seasoning, to taste

If you prefer to eat grain-free or low-carb, you can switch the breadcrumbs for some crushed pork scratchings or replace the wheat flour with polenta flour.

Homemade kievs are far nicer than shop-bought, and worth the extra effort. I like to use my own frozen garlic butter. Don't worry if you don't have any frozen garlic butter, you can easily make these with chilled butter.

First make the garlic butter: mix all the ingredients together until well combined. Place a sheet of cling film on your worktop and plop the butter mixture into the centre. Wrap to form into a sausage shape and either freeze if making in advance, or chill in the fridge while you prepare the chicken crust.

You now need three bowls – things are about to get messy! Add the flour to the first bowl. Beat the eggs well in the second bowl, then place the breadcrumbs, Parmesan (if using), parsley, oregano, paprika, onion granules and seasoning in the third bowl. Combine well.

Place the chicken onto your chopping board. Use a sharp knife and make a deep pocket into the breast, making sure you don't cut right the way through the chicken! (See page 77 for more information.)

Remove the garlic butter from the fridge or freezer. Cut into thick chunks and place 1 or 2 chunks into each of the chicken pockets. You need to try to ensure the chicken is sealed – you can use wooden cocktail sticks to help if you need to. Dipping it into the egg and crumb mixture will also give it a protective coating to prevent the butter leaking out.

Dip the chicken into the flour, then the egg mixture, then into the crumb mixture for the final time. You can pop these into the fridge to chill until you are ready to cook them.

Set your air fryer to 185°C. Place the chicken Kievs into your lined air fryer basket and cook for 20–25 minutes until golden. Timings can vary depending on the size of the chicken Kievs.

Chicken Ball Pittas

Serves 4-6

500g chicken mince

1 small onion, finely chopped

2 garlic cloves, crushed

1 chilli, finely chopped

½ tsp dried mint

½–1 tsp chilli powder

½ tsp ground cumin

1 tsp ground coriander

1 tsp dried thyme

pitta bread, tzatziki and salad, to serve

These chicken balls are perfect in stuffed pitta. Packed with protein and flavour, they can be cooked in advance and make the perfect light meal or packed lunch.

Place all the ingredients in a bowl and combine well.

Use your hands to form the mixture into 12 equal-sized balls and place these onto a plate. Refrigerate until you are ready to cook.

Place the chicken balls into the air fryer basket, ensuring they are not touching.

Set your air fryer to 190°C and cook for 15-20 minutes (in batches if necessary), shaking the basket regularly to ensure they are evenly coated and not sticking together.

Warm your pittas, before stuffing with salad and the chicken balls.

Asian-Inspired Chicken

Serves 4

500g skinless and boneless chicken (breast or thigh), diced

1 onion, finely diced

3 garlic cloves, crushed

3cm piece of fresh ginger, grated

2 red chillies, deseeded and finely chopped

1 tbsp rice wine vinegar

2 tbsp runny honey

2 tbsp brown sugar

3 tbsp sweet chilli sauce

2 tbsp tomato purée

4 tbsp dark soy sauce

To garnish

3-4 spring onions, finely chopped

small handful of sesame seeds

This is an easy take on Asian-style sticky chicken. It is a quick, bung-it-all-in type of meal, but tastes impressive, despite the little work it needs. Don't forget to top it with the sesame seeds and sliced spring onions – this really makes the dish come to life on the plate. I serve it with fluffy white rice, or, when I'm watching the carbs, cauliflower rice.

Place a silicone liner or an ovenproof dish into your air fryer basket. This is a wet recipe so the ingredients needs to be placed in something.

Combine the chicken, onion, garlic, ginger and chillies and place in the liner or ovenproof dish.

In a jug mix together the rice wine vinegar, honey, brown sugar, sweet chilli sauce, tomato purée and soy sauce. Pour this onto the chicken and combine well.

Set your air fryer to 170°C and cook for 20–25 minutes, stirring occasionally to ensure an even cook.

When ready to serve, finish with a garnish of sesame seeds and spring onions. Serve on a bed of rice.

Creamy Bacon & Thyme Chicken

Serves 4

4 skinless chicken breasts

2 garlic cloves, crushed

1 onion, finely diced

150g smoked pancetta, diced

150ml white wine

300ml double cream

2 tsp chicken seasoning

2–3 sprigs of fresh thyme

2 tsp dried oregano

1 tsp dried or freshly chopped parsley

seasoning, to taste

This is one of my family's favourite dishes and a very easy one to make; my husband virtually inhales this, he eats it so fast! I serve it with steamed green vegetables. It is very filling.

Place a liner in the base of the air fryer. If you don't have a liner, you can use an ovenproof dish; some air fryer baskets also allow you to remove the base, so you are cooking in the sealed basket.

Add the chicken, garlic, onion and pancetta, set your air fryer to 185°C and cook for 15 minutes.

Add the wine, cream, chicken seasoning, herbs and some salt and pepper and combine well. Cook for another 10 minutes, or until the chicken is completely cooked through. Stir occasionally to ensure an even cook.

Serve the chicken, with the delicious sauce covering it, with steamed seasonal green vegetables.

Chicken Schnitzel

Serves 4

400g skinless chicken breasts

100g plain flour

2 eggs, beaten

75g fine breadcrumbs

50g Parmesan cheese, grated

2 tsp paprika

1 tsp dried parsley

½ tsp dried oregano

seasoning, to taste

If you are feeling a bit stressed, grab your rolling pin and bash some chicken breasts to make these tasty chicken schnitzels. They work brilliantly in the air fryer and have the added bonus that kids love helping you make them – although it can get messy!

Place your chicken breasts on a board. You can butterfly any that are particularly large if you wish or simply cut them lengthways. Using a tenderising hammer or a rolling pin bash the chicken between sheets of parchment or cling film until the breast is flattened. You may want to cut these into a smaller size, especially if you are serving to children.

Add the flour to one bowl, the beaten eggs to a second bowl and in a third bowl combine the breadcrumbs, Parmesan, paprika, parsley and oregano. Season well.

Dip each chicken piece into the flour, then the eggs and then into the breadcrumb mixture, pressing gently to coat both sides.

Carefully place the chicken into the air fryer basket, ensuring the pieces are not overlapping. You may need to do this in batches if you have a small air fryer.

Set your air fryer to 190°C and cook for 15–20 minutes, or until golden brown. The timings will depend on the thickness of the chicken. Turn the chicken halfway through to ensure a good even cook.

Serve immediately.

Tandoori-Style Chicken

Serves 4

1 red onion, finely chopped

2–3 garlic cloves, crushed

1–2 chillies, finely chopped

1 tsp ground coriander

1 tsp ground cumin

3–4 tsp curry powder or garam masala

2 tsp ground turmeric

1 tsp ground cinnamon

2–3 tsp paprika

2.5cm piece of fresh ginger

zest and juice of 1 lemon

splash of olive oil

300ml Greek yoghurt

700g bone-in chicken pieces (thighs and drumsticks)

Tandoori chicken is a classic Indian dish that is made by marinating chicken in a yoghurt-based sauce flavoured with spices. The chicken is then cooked in a very hot clay oven. The air fryer can be a great option to make lovely tandoori-style chicken, although the chicken does need to marinate, so you'll need to plan this recipe in advance.

To make the marinade, place all the ingredients except for the chicken into your food processor and whizz until combined.

Place the chicken pieces in a sealable freezer bag and pour over the tandoori marinade. Seal the top and combine thoroughly, squishing the marinade into the chicken with your hands. For the best flavour, leave these to marinate for a few hours or overnight in the fridge (the longer you leave it the more intense the flavours).

Set your air fryer to 175°C. Place the chicken pieces into the basket. Cook for 20–25 minutes (timings will depend on the size of the chicken pieces), turning occasionally to ensure an even cook.

When the chicken is cooked, remove from the air fryer and serve hot or cold.

Creamy Garlic & Spinach Stuffed Chicken

Serves 2

2 skinless chicken breasts

150g garlic and herb soft cheese (I use Boursin)

60g baby leaf spinach

½ tsp grated nutmeg (optional)

1–2 tsp olive oil

seasoning, to taste

This is so easy to make but so delicious. Serve it with steamed vegetables in the winter months but it's also perfect for a summer's evening with a selection of salads. It is a bit of a cheat as we use garlic and herb soft cheese to stuff the chicken.

Use a sharp knife to cut into the chicken breasts lengthways, making sure you don't cut all the way through so that you retain a little seam, like opening a book. This will enable you to stuff the chicken breast.

Add the soft cheese to a bowl and soften with a fork. Place the spinach in a colander or sieve and run under hot water until it starts to wilt slightly – this makes it easier to stir into the cheese. Drain really well, pressing the spinach against the colander or sieve to remove any excess water, then pat dry with kitchen towel and add to the cheese. Stir until well combined, then season generously and add some grated nutmeg.

Stuff this mixture into the chicken breasts.

Brush the tops of the chicken breasts with a little olive oil before placing into the air fryer. You can place this on a piece of baking parchment if you want to avoid mess (there might be some seepage).

Set your air fryer to 185°C and cook for 20–30 minutes (depending on size of the chicken breast), until the chicken is cooked through and nice and golden.

Serve with steamed vegetables or a delicious salad.

4

Meat

In this chapter you'll find a selection of delicious meat dishes using beef, lamb and pork. These recipes are all family favourites and do check out the side dishes chapter as you'll find plenty of recipes that you can combine with the recipes here to create a complete meal.

Toad in the Hole

Serves 4

1 tbsp olive oil, goose fat,
duck fat or beef dripping

8 sausages

250ml milk

1 large egg

150g plain flour

seasoning, to taste

This is such a lovely family-friendly dish and so easy to make. There are many options to cook this in the air fryer. You can remove the inner tray and cook on the base, or you can do what I do and place an ovenproof dish into the basket, but it depends on the size and shape of your air fryer. You can also make individual toad in the holes, using smaller dishes, such as tin foil trays. You can use a silicone liner, but I would recommend you do this only if you have the sturdier liners with handles, as the thinner ones can struggle with removing and serving toad in the hole.

Set your air fryer to 185°C.

Place the ovenproof dish into your air fryer basket (or see above advice) and add the oil and sausages. Cook for 10–12 minutes until the sausages are starting to brown evenly. You may want to shake them during the cooking time.

In a large bowl, whisk together the milk and egg. Gradually add the flour and continue to whisk until it is all combined. Season with salt and pepper.

Keeping the sausages in the dish or basket, pour the batter over the sausages. It may spit a little at first, but it needs to be done when very hot.

Place back into the air fryer and cook for another 10–15 minutes, or until the batter is golden brown, especially in the centre.

Serve immediately with some mashed potato and vegetables.

Beef Lasagne

Serves 4-6

4-6 fresh lasagne sheets

For the mince base

1 tbsp olive oil

1 onion, chopped

2 garlic cloves, very finely chopped

1 red pepper, deseeded and finely diced

100g lardons or pancetta (optional)

500g beef mince

300ml beef stock or red wine

400g tin chopped tomatoes

2 tbsp tomato purée

75g mushrooms, roughly chopped

1 tsp paprika

1 tsp dried oregano

1 tsp dried basil

½ tsp salt

¼ tsp ground black pepper

For the easy white sauce

400g crème fraîche

100g Cheddar cheese, grated

100ml milk or 1 small egg (optional)

50g Parmesan cheese, grated

You can't have an everyday family cookbook without including a lovely beef lasagne. I recommend you double the recipe of the mince mixture, as it makes a perfect bolognese for another meal, which can be frozen or kept in the fridge for up to 2-3 days.

Heat the olive oil in a sauté pan, add the onion and fry until soft and translucent. Add the garlic and pepper and cook for another couple of minutes.

Add the lardons (if using) and mince and cook until brown, then add the stock or wine and cook for 2 more minutes.

Stir in the chopped tinned tomatoes, then add the mushrooms, paprika, herbs and salt and pepper. Leave to simmer very gently for 10 minutes.

Meanwhile, combine the crème fraîche and grated Cheddar. You can add a little milk or beat in a small egg if you want to slacken the mixture as it can sometimes get a bit too thick to spread on the layers.

Add a layer of the beef mixture to the bottom of a lasagne dish or your silicone liner. Cover with a layer of the white sauce, followed by a layer of lasagne sheets. Continue this process once more, ending with a final layer of white sauce.

Scatter the grated Parmesan over the final layer and sprinkle with black pepper.

Set your air fryer to 180°C. Place the lasagne in your basket and cook for 15-20 minutes until golden and bubbling. Please adjust this temperature and time if you are using dried lasagne sheets (see Note opposite).

Serve with salad and garlic bread.

When making a lasagne in an air fryer, I recommend using fresh pasta sheets. This cuts down on the cooking time but also ensures you get perfectly cooked lasagne. If you use lasagne sheets where no pre-cooking is required, you need to cook at a lower temperature (160°C) for 30–35 minutes.

NOTE

This is a wet dish so you will need to cook this in a silicone liner or in an ovenproof dish.

Roast Beef with Horseradish

Serves 4-6

4 tbsp horseradish sauce or Dijon or wholegrain mustard

1kg boneless beef joint

ground black pepper

1 red onion, roughly chopped

1 large carrot, roughly chopped

NOTE

Timings are approximate, and this recipe is aimed at producing beef that is medium-rare. You will need to adjust the timings depending on the size of joint, your machine and how you like your beef. I recommend using a meat thermometer, which you push into the centre of the joint to assess cooking time. An approximate guide is to cook until 50°C for rare; 60°C for medium; and 70°C for well done.

We all love a good roast dinner. If you are lucky enough to have a dual basket air fryer, you can cook your meat in one drawer and your roast potatoes in the other, saving money by not having to use a conventional oven. I love my beef on the rare side, but please follow the advice below to adjust timings to your personal taste.

Spread the horseradish or mustard all over the joint and season well with black pepper.

Place the onion and carrot into the base of the air fryer basket before adding the beef joint. Set your air fryer to 180°C and cook for 15 minutes before reducing the temperature to 170°C and cooking for another 30–40 minutes (see Note).

Once cooked, remove from the oven, wrap in foil, and leave to rest for at least 20 minutes. Use this time to make your gravy using any of the natural juices that have gathered in the base of the basket.

Serve with roast potatoes (see page 174), Yorkshire puddings (see page 173) and steamed vegetables.

Simple Gammon Joint

Serves 4–5

1kg gammon joint

1–2 tbsp honey (optional)

seasoning, to taste

There is nothing nicer than a fresh home-cooked gammon joint and it is also so much cheaper than buying sliced gammon or ham from the deli counter. This is a no-frills recipe, but you can of course treat the gammon joint to some wholegrain mustard, cloves or whatever coating or glaze you prefer.

Place the gammon joint in the centre of a large piece of foil. Place your chosen glaze onto the gammon. I simply brush it with honey and season to taste.

Wrap the gammon in the foil and seal tightly.

Set your air fryer to 180°C. Place the gammon into the air fryer and cook for 30 minutes.

Remove the foil, return the gammon to the air fryer basket and cook for an additional 15–20 minutes (depending on the size of the gammon joint). To check if the gammon is cooked, it needs to have reached an internal temperature of 62°C. You can test this with a meat thermometer.

Once cooked, remove from the air fryer. You can either serve this hot, or leave to cool completely before placing into an airtight container and storing in the fridge, ready to slice up as needed.

Pork Chops with Creamy Garlic Sauce

Serves 4

4 pork chops

olive oil, for brushing

seasoning, to taste

For the sauce

1 tbsp butter

1–2 garlic cloves, crushed

75ml white wine

250ml double cream

1 chicken stock cube
(I use gel stock)

1 tsp dried thyme

seasoning, to taste

This recipe has a delicious creamy sauce that works perfectly with pork. The sauce is made separately so you can of course use this recipe just to make your favourite pork chops without the sauce if you prefer. If you like the sauce, it does freeze well so you can double up the batch and freeze half for another day.

Brush the pork chops with some olive oil. Season to taste.

Place the pork chops into your air fryer basket, ensuring they don't overlap.

Set your air fryer to 185°C and cook for 10–14 minutes, depending on the size and thickness of the pork chop.

While the pork chops are cooking, you can get on with making the sauce. Put the butter and garlic into a saucepan and cook over a medium heat for 2–3 minutes.

Add the wine and cook for another minute before adding the cream, stock cube, thyme and seasoning. Cook over a medium heat for 5 minutes, then turn to low and keep it warm until the pork chops are ready.

Once the pork chops are cooked, place the sauce into a serving jug. Serve immediately.

Serve with new potatoes, steamed vegetables and the creamy sauce.

Chilli Con Carne

Serves 4

1 red onion, finely chopped

2 garlic cloves, crushed

1 star anise

1 red pepper, deseeded and diced

1–2 chillies, deseeded and chopped

150g chorizo, chopped (optional)

1 tbsp olive oil

500g lean minced beef

1 tsp ground cumin

1 tsp ground coriander

1 tsp chilli powder

1 tsp smoked paprika

2 tsp dried marjoram

1 beef stock cube (I use gel stock)

400g tin chopped tomatoes

400g tin kidney beans, drained and rinsed

1 tbsp tomato purée

150ml water

1 square of dark chocolate (optional)

seasoning, to taste

My husband loves a chilli, so this is a regular feature in our house. This recipe is somewhere between moderately spicy and hot, so if you prefer a milder chilli, do adjust the seasoning to taste. It is lovely served on a bed of rice, but we also like to serve it with some Parmesan crisps and a pot of sour cream.

Add the onion, garlic, star anise, red pepper, chillies and chorizo (if using) to a liner or ovenproof dish (or direct into the base of the basket). Drizzle with the olive oil.

Set your air fryer to 185°C and cook for 5 minutes, or until the vegetables are softened, then add the minced beef and cook for 5 minutes, or until browned.

Stir in the spices, herbs and stock and season with salt and pepper.

Add the chopped tomatoes, kidney beans and tomato purée. Add the water as required – you may not need to use it all. Combine well.

Reduce the temperature to 175°C and cook for another 10–15 minutes, stirring occasionally until the chilli is thickened. Add the dark chocolate (if using) and stir until is melted through the chilli.

Serve on a bed of rice.

Warm Marinated Steak Salad

Serves 2

1 tbsp Dijon mustard

2 tsp Worcestershire sauce

½ tsp garlic powder

300g steak (rump, ribeye or sirloin)

seasoning, to taste

For the simple salad

½ red onion, sliced
(or use spring onions)

¼ cucumber, sliced

8 cherry tomatoes, halved

2 handfuls of green salad leaves

For the dressing

2 tbsp extra virgin olive oil

2 tbsp red wine vinegar

1 tsp Dijon mustard

½ tsp honey

seasoning, to taste

This is so simple but tastes amazing. You can cook the steak without marinating it first, but I find that even a few hours in the marinade really does improve the flavours. I add my sliced steak to a very straightforward salad, but you can add whatever you like to your salad. It's also great when topped with crumbled blue cheese.

Combine the mustard, Worcestershire sauce, garlic powder and some salt and pepper in a small bowl, then rub this mixture all over the steak. Leave to marinate in the fridge for at least 2 hours, or up to overnight.

When you are ready to cook, set your air fryer to 185°C and place the steak in the air fryer basket. Cook for 10–12 minutes for medium-rare, depending on thickness, or until it is cooked to your desired doneness.

While the steak is cooking, prepare your simple salad and add to a serving bowl.

Make the dressing by whisking together the olive oil, red wine vinegar, Dijon mustard, honey and some salt and pepper in a small bowl.

When the steak is cooked, let it rest for a few minutes before slicing.

Add the steak to the salad and toss to coat, then serve immediately with the dressing on the side.

Lamb Burgers

Serves 4

500g lamb mince

1 onion, finely chopped

1 small piece of fresh ginger, peeled and finely grated

2 garlic cloves, crushed

1–2 red chillies, deseeded and finely chopped

handful of fresh coriander, chopped

handful of fresh parsley, chopped

1 tsp ground cumin

1 tsp ground coriander

seasoning, to taste

vegetables, to serve

A lovely alternative to beef burgers, which work brilliantly in the air fryer. You can put them in your favourite burger bun, but I prefer to have these with salad, tzatziki sauce and some warm pitta.

In a large bowl, combine the minced lamb with the onion, ginger, garlic and chilli. Mix well to combine. Add the herbs and spices and season. Mix again.

Form the lamb mixture into four burger shapes. I find the easiest way to do this is to make a ball and then flatten it.

Place the lamb burgers into the air fryer basket, ensuring they are not overlapping. Set the temperature to 190°C and cook for 10–12 minutes, or until cooked through.

Serve immediately on a bed of vegetables.

The Everyday Family Air Fryer Cookbook

Stuffed Loin of Pork

Serves 4

75g breadcrumbs

1 red onion, finely chopped

2–3 garlic cloves, finely chopped

200g smoked lardons or pancetta, diced

50g pine nuts

70g dried cranberries

handful of thyme sprigs, leaves stripped from stalks and finely chopped

500g pork tenderloin fillet

olive oil

seasoning, to taste

Pork tenderloin makes an absolutely delicious meal. You can stuff it with whatever you fancy really. In this recipe, I have packed it with my favourite flavours, including some dried cranberries, which are available all year around so make the most of them! They give a nice sweetness to the stuffing.

Put the breadcrumbs, onion, garlic, bacon, pine nuts, cranberries and chopped thyme into a bowl. Combine well and season to taste.

Prepare the pork loin for stuffing (if you have a local butcher you could ask them to do this for you). Using a sharp knife, cut the long side of the loin about two-thirds in so you can then open it up, like opening a book. You will end up with a rectangle of meat. You can use a meat hammer if you want to bash it down slightly, but this is not necessary.

Place the stuffing down the centre of the meat, leaving a gap around the edges, and roll up tightly. Use water-soaked string or butcher's twine to tie the loin up securely at roughly 2–3cm intervals.

Rub the skin with olive oil and sprinkle with sea salt and black pepper.

Place the stuffed loin in the basket. Set your air fryer to 190°C and cook for 20–30 minutes before turning down the temperature to 170°C and cooking for a further 20–30 minutes, or until the internal temperature of the joint reaches 60–65°C.

Leave to rest for 10–15 minutes before carving.

Crispy Pork Belly

Serves 4-6

1kg deboned pork belly, skin on

1 tbsp olive oil

seasoning, to taste

I also leave my pork belly uncovered (and unseasoned) in the fridge overnight the night before cooking, which helps dry out the skin a little more – the drier the skin the crispier it will be.

The air fryer works brilliantly when it comes to making a really crispy pork belly. Here the pork is just seasoned, leaving the air fryer to do all the work. You can adjust the cooking times depending on how 'crisp' you want the pork belly.

Score the skin of the pork belly in straight lines . Using some kitchen towel, rub the skin to ensure it is very dry.

Rub the pork belly all over with olive oil and season. I tend to be quite heavy-handed with both salt and pepper here.

Set your air fryer to 160°C. Place the pork belly in the air fryer basket and cook for 40 minutes, then turn the heat up to 195°C and cook for an additional 10–20 minutes, depending on your desired crispness.

Let the pork belly rest for 10 minutes before slicing and serving.

The Everyday Family Air Fryer Cookbook

Lamb Koftas

**Serves 4
(makes up to 12 koftas)**

500g lamb mince

1 tsp ground cumin

2 tsp paprika

1 tsp ground turmeric

2 tsp ground coriander

1 tsp ground cinnamon

1 tsp chilli powder

1 red chilli, finely chopped

1 red onion, very finely chopped

1 tbsp tomato purée

small handful of coriander leaves, finely chopped

seasoning, to taste

These wonderful Greek koftas take me back to a holiday in Kefalonia. They are great served hot with some soft pittas for a lovey evening meal, or you can enjoy them cold in a packed lunch. They also freeze brilliantly before or after cooking.

Place the mince in a large bowl and break it up with your hands. Add all the remaining ingredients and mix thoroughly until evenly combined.

Form into fat sausage shapes, place on a tray lined with baking parchment and pop into the fridge for 30 minutes to chill.

When ready to cook, set your air fryer to 180°C. Cook the koftas for 25–30 minutes, turning them regularly to ensure an even cook.

I like to serve these on skewers, which I insert after cooking, while they are still warm, but this is optional.

5

Fish & Seafood

Here are a handful of fish recipes to get your started on your air fryer journey. Fish tends to need a shorter cooking time than meat, so the air fryer is perfect for this. My favourite recipe is the Herby Cod, but do let me know yours. The Quick & Easy Garlic & Chilli Prawns on page 140 are great for a quick meal and work beautifully stirred into pasta as an alternative way of serving.

Salmon, Potato & Chilli Fishcakes

Serves 4

100g breadcrumbs

1 tbsp semolina

1 heaped tbsp finely grated Parmesan

2 x 170g tins salmon

350g potatoes, peeled, cooked and mashed (you can also use sweet potatoes)

3 spring onions, finely chopped

1–2 chillies, finely chopped

1 tsp ground cumin

1 tbsp lemon juice

small handful of coriander leaves, finely chopped

2 eggs, beaten

plain flour, to bind (optional)

olive oil spray

seasoning, to taste

Salmon fishcakes are one of my mum's favourite meals. This is a very easy recipe, using tinned salmon, but you can use fresh salmon, as long as you cook it first. These fishcakes also freeze well before or after cooking. I pop mine between layers of parchment to stop them sticking together before popping them into the freezer. These can be cooked from frozen, but I advise lowering the temperature and cooking for longer, ensuring they are cooked thoroughly.

Combine the breadcrumbs, semolina and Parmesan, season and leave to one side.

Put the fish, mashed potato, spring onions, chillies, cumin, lemon juice and coriander into a large bowl and mix until combined. Add a little beaten egg to help bind the mixture only if needed. Season to taste.

Form the mixture into 4 fishcakes. If the mix is too wet, add a little plain flour. Once the cakes are formed, you can leave them to rest in the fridge until you are ready to cook or continue with the coating.

To coat the fishcakes, brush each one with a little beaten egg then dip into the breadcrumb mixture. This is a little messy so be prepared! Place on a sheet of greased baking parchment and chill in the fridge for 10 minutes.

Remove the fishcakes from the fridge, spray with a light coating of olive oil, being careful not to displace the breadcrumb topping.

Set your air fryer to 180°C. Place the fishcakes in the basket and cook for 10–12 minutes, turning them halfway through to ensure they are evenly cooked and browned.

Serve with a lovely green salad and lemon wedges to squeeze over.

Tuna & Sweetcorn Lasagne

Serves 4

400g tinned tuna in spring water (about 2 tins, drained), mashed

4 spring onions, chopped

200g sweetcorn (tinned or frozen)

250g tub of ricotta cheese

150g Cheddar cheese, grated

4–5 fresh lasagne sheets

40g Parmesan cheese, grated

seasoning, to taste

NOTE

When making a lasagne in the air fryer, I recommend using fresh pasta sheets. This cuts down on the cooking time but also ensures you get perfectly cooked lasagne. If you use lasagne sheets where no pre-cooking is required, you need to cook at a lower temperature (160°C) for 30–35 minutes.

This is a lovely change from the classic meat lasagne and kids love it. You'll need to cook this in a silicone liner or in an ovenproof dish.

Mix the tuna, spring onions and sweetcorn together in a bowl. Season to taste.

In a separate bowl, mix together the ricotta cheese and grated Cheddar.

Add a layer of tuna mash to the bottom of a lasagne dish or your silicone liner. Cover with a layer of the ricotta cheese mix, followed by half the lasagne sheets. Continue this process once more, ending with a final layer of the ricotta.

Add the grated Parmesan over the final layer of ricotta and sprinkle with black pepper.

Set your air fryer to 180°C. Place the lasagne in your basket and cook for 15–20 minutes until golden and bubbling. Please adjust this temperature and time if you are using dried lasagne sheets (see Note).

Serve with salad and garlic bread.

Homemade Fish Fingers

Serves 4-6

50g breadcrumbs

75g either cornflakes or pork scratchings, crushed

50g Parmesan cheese, grated

1 tsp dried parsley

1 tsp dried oregano

½ tsp onion salt

zest of 1 lemon

1 egg

500g cod or pollock fillets

seasoning, to taste

Kids love fish fingers, but there's no need to buy the processed frozen ones from the supermarket. These easy homemade alternatives are far tastier and healthier. You can get the kids to help you make them too, as they're so simple. Even better: they can be prepared in advance and frozen. There are three options for the coating – breadcrumbs are traditional but cornflakes or pork scratchings (ideal for those who eat grain-free or low-carb) also give that perfect crunchy texture.

Combine the breadcrumbs, cornflakes or pork scratchings, Parmesan, parsley, oregano, onion salt and lemon zest in a bowl and season to taste.

Beat the egg in another bowl.

Place your fish fillets onto your chopping board and use a sharp knife to cut them into thick fingers.

Dip the fish fingers into the egg mixture, then into the breadcrumb mixture.

Set your air fryer to 190°C. Place the fish fingers into the air fryer basket and cook for 15–20 minutes until golden, turning halfway to ensure an even crispy coating.

Herby Cod

Serves 4

small handful of fresh herbs
(I use basil, thyme and parsley)

zest, juice and thin slices of
½ lemon

1–2 garlic cloves

2 tbsp olive oil

4 plump cod fillets

seasoning, to taste

This is so simple but tastes amazing. I have used my favourite herbs with this dish, but you can opt for any you fancy. Always use fresh herbs, as dried won't have the same impact. You can use frozen cod fillets for this if you don't have fresh, although they will need to be defrosted before cooking.

Place the herbs, lemon zest and juice, garlic and olive oil in a food processor and whizz until they form a paste. Season to taste.

Spread the herb paste over the cod fillets and place the lemon slices on top.

Set your air fryer to 185°C, then place the cod fillets into the air fryer and cook for 10–15 minutes, depending on the thickness of the fillets, until the fish flakes easily.

The Everyday Family Air Fryer Cookbook

Loaded Salad Niçoise

Serves 4

8–12 new potatoes

4 hard-boiled eggs (see Note)

4 tuna steaks

olive oil, for brushing

6 asparagus tips

80g salad or spinach leaves

8–10 cherry tomatoes, halved

1 small red onion, thinly sliced

60g pitted black olives

salad dressing, for drizzling

NOTE

If you have a dual basket air fryer you can, of course, use it to cook your boiled eggs – see page 23 for more information.

This is one of my favourite salads – it's packed with goodness and is an absolute delight. You can, of course, use tinned tuna, but once you have experienced the delights of fresh tuna steaks, there really is no going back. You can also use frozen tuna steaks in this recipe, just adjust the timings slightly if you are cooking from frozen, but keep to the same times if you have defrosted the tuna.

Place your new potatoes on to steam, this should take 15–20 minutes depending on the size of the potatoes.

While the potatoes are cooking, boil your eggs. Once cooked, remove from the heat and immediately run the eggs under cold water – this helps them peel easily and also stops them continuing to cook.

Brush your tuna steaks with a little olive oil.

Set your air fryer to 180°C. Place the tuna steaks in the air fryer basket and cook for 4–6 minutes, depending on the thickness. Fresh tuna should be nice and pink in the middle, so take care not to overcook it.

Meanwhile, blanch your asparagus tips in the boiling water of the steamer for 3–5 minutes. Remove and plunge into cold water.

Add the salad or spinach leaves to a serving platter and add the asparagus, sliced new potatoes, tomatoes, onion and olives.

Remove the tuna from the air fryer and cut into thick slices. Add this to the salad. Peel the hard-boiled eggs then cut them into quarters and add to the salad, then finish with a drizzle of your favourite dressing. Serve immediately.

Quick & Easy Garlic & Chilli Prawns

Serves 2

400g peeled and deveined large raw prawns, with tails left on

1 tbsp olive oil

2 garlic cloves, crushed

1–2 red chillies, finely chopped

½ tsp chilli flakes (optional)

zest and juice of 1 lemon

seasoning, to taste

small handful of chopped fresh parsley, to garnish

This really is a fantastically quick recipe, leaving you free to prepare whatever you wish to eat with the prawns. You could have them with a salad or mix them into a pasta dish. They are also lovely on their own with some dipping sauce. I like good strong flavours, so please adjust the garlic and chilli quantities if you prefer a milder flavour.

In a large bowl, combine the prawns with the olive oil, garlic, chilli and lemon zest and juice. Season well and ensure everything is evenly coated. You can either cook this immediately or leave in the fridge to marinate for at least 1 hour until you are ready to eat.

Set your air fryer to 190°C, place the prawns in the air fryer basket and cook for 5–7 minutes, or until pink and cooked through. You will need to give the basket a shake once or twice during the cooking time to ensure they cook evenly.

Garnish with the fresh parsley and serve immediately.

The Everyday Family Air Fryer Cookbook

Butter & Herb Salmon Parcels

Serves 2

2 garlic cloves

small handful of basil leaves

few sprigs of parsley

50g butter, plus extra for greasing

2 salmon fillets, skin on (about 125g each)

ground pepper and peppercorns, to taste

juice of 1 lemon

Some people don't like strong flavours with salmon as they can overpower it, but I adore this recipe, and it's especially good to prepare up to a day in advance in the fridge. The herby butter creates the most amazing sauce to accompany the salmon.

Place the garlic, herbs and butter in a food processor and whizz until combined.

Butter two large squares of foil or baking parchment. Place the salmon in the centre of the foil or parchment.

Brush the herb paste over the salmon and season with ground pepper and peppercorns. Drizzle with some lemon juice if you wish or you can leave this until serving.

Bring up the sides of the foil or parchment around the salmon and fold to make a parcel, making sure the edges are sealed well.

Set your air fryer to 185°C, place the foil parcels in the air fryer basket and cook for 10–15 minutes until the fish flakes easily. Serve immediately.

6

Vegan & Vegetarian

More and more people are opting for plant-based diets or choosing to go vegan or vegetarian on certain days of the week, so here are a few of my favourite recipes. You can swap some of the ingredients to make vegetarian dishes vegan if you wish – for example, milk can be changed to your preferred dairy-free milk with ease. Cheese substitutes are easy to find in shops but do look at the ingredients as often these can be highly processed and full of inflammatory oils, so choose wisely. I am a big fan of nutritional yeast flakes, which are packed with B vitamins and add a 'cheesy' flavour to meals, making them perfect for vegans. I have published a book called *The Part-Time Vegan*, so do check this out if you are looking for more vegan recipes.

Baked Stuffed Aubergines

Serves 4

2 aubergines

1–2 tbsp olive oil

1 onion, diced

1 red pepper, deseeded and diced

2 garlic cloves, diced

150g cherry tomatoes, quartered

2–3 tbsp sundried tomato paste

1 tsp paprika

1 tsp dried oregano

seasoning, to taste

If you are not vegan, you can top the stuffed aubergines with your favourite grated cheese before baking.

This is a great dish which can be prepared in advance and left in the fridge until you're ready to bake it. You can use the same recipe to stuff peppers, butternut squash or large beefsteak tomatoes.

Cut the aubergines in half lengthways. Remove some of the flesh from the centre so it can be stuffed and set this to one side.

Brush the aubergine shells with a little of the olive oil and season well with salt and pepper. Set aside.

Heat the remaining olive oil in a sauté pan over a medium heat. Add the diced onion, red pepper and garlic and cook until they start to soften.

Add the aubergine flesh that you removed from the halved aubergines, cherry tomatoes, sundried tomato paste, paprika and oregano, season to taste and cook for 5–10 minutes until softened.

Stuff the aubergines with the sauté mixture and place them into the air fryer. You may have to do this in batches depending on the size of your basket. Set the temperature to 180°C and cook for 12–15 minutes.

Serve with a lovely green salad.

The Best Nut Roast

Serves 6

1 tbsp olive oil

1 onion, finely chopped

2 garlic cloves, crushed

125g Brazil nuts, finely chopped

125g cashews, finely chopped

250g mushrooms, finely chopped

1 tbsp yeast extract

1 tsp dried oregano

25g ground almonds

1 large carrot, grated

75g dried cranberries

seasoning, to taste

This is a fantastic recipe for a veggie roast or Christmas dinner and has been popular with meat eaters and vegetarians alike. Having a food processor to chop the nuts really does speed up the preparation process.

Heat the olive oil in a frying pan over a medium heat. Add the onion and garlic and fry for a few minutes until translucent but not browned.

Add the nuts and mushrooms and cook for 5 minutes.

Add the yeast extract and oregano, followed by the ground almonds and grated carrot. Season to taste before stirring in the dried cranberries.

Place into a silicone loaf tin (ensuring it fits into your air fryer) and press down to form a firm base. If your air fryer is not big enough, you can cook the mixture in small ramekin dishes and serve as individual portions.

Set your air fryer to 180°C and cook for 20 minutes. If using small ramekins, adjust the timing and test them after 12–15 minutes.

Once cooked, remove your loaf tin or ramekins from the air fryer and turn out onto your serving plate.

Spiced Tofu Burgers

Serves 6

400g tin chickpeas, drained and rinsed

400g pack firm organic tofu, crumbled

1–2 tbsp plant-based milk alternative (optional)

olive oil, for frying

1 onion, finely chopped

1–2 garlic cloves, crushed

1 red chilli, finely chopped

1 celery stick, finely chopped

1 tbsp sundried tomato paste

1–3 tsp garam masala

splash of vegan soy sauce

2 tsp paprika

1 tsp dried oregano

2–4 tbsp polenta flour

seasoning, to taste

Who doesn't love a burger? These vegan burgers are really simple to make and I thoroughly recommend you make a double batch and freeze half for another day. Remember to freeze them with baking parchment separating each burger to prevent them sticking together.

Tip the chickpeas into a large bowl and mash until soft. Add the tofu and continue to mash until mixed thoroughly. You may need to add a little plant-based milk to encourage the mixture to form a good mash. Don't overdo this: 1–2 tablespoons is all you'll need. Set aside.

Meanwhile, add a small amount of olive oil to a sauté pan and fry the onion, garlic, chilli and celery over a medium heat until soft. Remove from heat and add to the chickpea and tofu mixture.

Add the sundried tomato paste, garam masala, soy sauce, herbs and spices. Season well. Add the polenta flour a little at a time. You may not need all this; it is only to help bind the mixture to form burger shapes.

The burgers are now ready. You can place them the fridge or freezer until ready to use (if freezing, separate with baking parchment to prevent them sticking together).

When ready to cook, set your air fryer to 180°C and place the burgers in the air fryer basket, ensuring they are not overlapping. Cook for 5 minutes, before turning them and cooking for another 5 minutes until both sides are golden.

Serve in seeded baps, along with salad, red onion, pickles and your sauces of choice.

Roast Vegetable Salad with Feta

Serves 4

100g dried brown lentils (you can use ready-cooked from a tin or pouch if you prefer)

2 small beetroots, scrubbed and trimmed and cut into wedges

1 large sweet potato, peeled and cut into thick wedges

1 tbsp olive oil

1 tbsp balsamic vinegar

small handful of fresh mint leaves, finely chopped

juice of ½ lemon

3 spring onions, very finely chopped

150g feta cheese, crumbled

extra virgin olive oil, for drizzling

fresh parsley and pomegranate seeds, to garnish

seasoning, to taste

This is a delicious salad, served on a bed of brown lentils. I am using beetroot and sweet potato, but you can use any roasted vegetable you like. The sweetness of the roasted vegetables really complements the flavours of the feta and minted brown lentils. If you are vegan, you can omit the feta and perhaps swap it for some tofu or tempeh.

Cook your lentils in boiling water until soft. Drain and leave to one side. (You can skip this step if you are using ready-cooked lentils from a tin or pouch.)

While the lentils are cooking, place the beetroot and the sweet potato in a lined air fryer basket. Drizzle with the olive oil and balsamic vinegar and season to taste.

Set your air fryer to 185°C and cook the vegetables for 15–20 minutes until soft.

Remove from the air fryer and start to assemble your salad.

Place the lentils in a large serving bowl and stir in the mint leaves, lemon juice and spring onions until well mixed.

Add the roasted vegetables and finish with the crumbled feta cheese. Drizzle with some extra virgin olive oil and garnish with parsley and pomegranate seeds before serving.

The Everyday Family Air Fryer Cookbook

Garlic, Herb & Cherry Tomato Pasta Bake

Serves 4

150g garlic and herb soft cheese (I use Boursin)

1 small onion, finely chopped

100g cherry tomatoes

300g penne pasta

75g Parmesan cheese, grated, plus extra to serve

seasoning, to taste

fresh parsley, chopped, to serve

This is such an easy recipe. You add it all in the dish or straight into your air fryer basket and allow it to bake. A few stirs later and you have a delicious meal with minimal effort. What could be better?

Put the cheese, onion and cherry tomatoes into the air fryer basket. This can be either directly into the base, or you can use a silicone liner or an ovenproof dish.

Set your air fryer to 180°C and cook for 10 minutes.

Meanwhile, cook your pasta according to the packet instructions. Drain, reserving 2 tablespoons of the pasta water.

Remove the tomato and cheese mixture from the air fryer. Stir until everything is combined nicely.

Add the pasta to the cheese and tomato mixture and stir until it is well combined. Season well. Use some of the pasta water to help if it needs to be a bit looser.

Cover with the grated Parmesan and return to the air fryer for another 8–10 minutes until heated through.

Serve with a sprinkle of fresh parsley and some extra Parmesan. This is also delicious with some feta crumbled over the top.

Cauliflower & Broccoli Bake

Serves 2

250g cauliflower and broccoli florets

1 tbsp butter

1 tbsp plain flour

350ml milk

125g extra mature Cheddar cheese, grated, plus extra to top

½ tsp mustard powder (optional)

1 tbsp nutritional yeast flakes (optional)

seasoning, to taste

This is one of my all-time favourite comfort foods. I love anything with a cheese sauce, while my husband, on the other hand, absolutely hates anything with cheese in it. For that reason this has become my guilty pleasure for mealtimes when it is just me.

Place the cauliflower and broccoli florets into your steamer and steam until just starting to soften – you want them a little al dente, so they hold their shape after being baked. I always prefer to steam veg as it preserves the nutrients and it also means the cauliflower doesn't get too wet, which can affect the cheese sauce.

While the cauliflower and broccoli are cooking, start on the sauce by melting the butter over a medium heat in a saucepan. Add the flour and stir well with your wooden spoon for 1 minute. Switch to a balloon whisk before gradually starting to add the milk, whisking all the time as the milk is added. It will slowly start to thicken and become smooth. Once at the desired thickness, add the grated cheese and mustard powder and yeast flakes (if using). Season well to taste, then remove from the heat.

When the florets are ready, place them into your ovenproof dish, ensuring it fits into your air fryer basket. Pour over the sauce. You can finish with some extra grated cheese if you wish. If you are cooking this in advance, you can place it in the fridge or freezer until you are ready to bake.

Set your air fryer to 185°C, place the ovenproof dish into the air fryer and bake for 10 minutes. (If you are cooking this straight from the fridge, increase the cooking time by 5–10 minutes to ensure it is evenly heated all the way through.) You can turn down the heat a little if it gets too dark on top.

Serve immediately.

Side Dishes

This chapter is all about the side dishes: accompaniments that can really elevate your meals, from classics such as Roast Potatoes, Yorkshire Puddings and Pigs in Blankets to roasted veg, corn on the cob and many more. You will also find recipes that can be turned into a meal in their own right, such as my Loaded Jacket Potatoes or Roasted Fennel and Chickpea Salad.

Roasted Potato Salad

Serves 4

1kg baby new potatoes, cleaned and thickly sliced

1–2 tbsp olive oil

½ tsp onion powder

2 garlic cloves, crushed

½ tsp paprika

small handful of radishes, sliced

1 bunch of spring onions, diced

1 tbsp wholegrain mustard

small handful of flat-leaf parsley, roughly chopped

I adore this dish – I've been known to serve this as a main meal with some hard-boiled eggs thrown in along with some diced feta cheese. It is also delicious with some pancetta or lardons added.

Place the sliced potatoes into a bowl. Mix the olive oil, onion powder, garlic and paprika together and pour this over the potatoes. Combine well until the potatoes are evenly coated in the oil.

Set your air fryer to 190°C, place the potatoes into the air fryer basket and cook for 20–30 minutes until the potatoes are golden. Shake a few times during cooking to ensure an even cook.

Remove the potatoes from the air fryer and tip into a serving bowl. Add all the remaining ingredients, combine well and serve immediately.

Roasted Courgettes with Parmesan

Serves 4

2 courgettes, thickly sliced

2 tbsp olive oil

½ tsp onion powder

½ tsp garlic powder

½ tsp paprika

½ tsp dried oregano

40g Parmesan cheese,
finely grated (optional)

seasoning, to taste

I love these. Courgette is really underrated, and this recipe is so delicious, you will be begging for more. It has a rich, sharp edge thanks to the Parmesan, but you can omit this if you prefer. Remember to shake the courgettes regularly to ensure they crisp up nicely.

Place the sliced courgettes in a bowl.

Mix the olive oil with the spices and oregano, then season with salt and pepper.

Pour this mix over the courgettes and combine well, ensuring they are evenly covered. If you prefer, you can brush a little on each slice, but this takes longer. Scatter over the Parmesan (if using).

Set your air fryer to 190°C, place the courgettes in the air fryer basket and cook for 10-12 minutes, shaking regularly during cooking to ensure an even cook.

Serve immediately.

Easy Cheesy Garlic Bread

Serves 2

1 French baguette or similar

75g unsalted butter, softened

3 garlic cloves, finely chopped or grated

15g Parmesan cheese, grated

1 tsp dried parsley

40g Cheddar cheese (optional), grated

seasoning, to taste

Who doesn't love garlic bread? You can use any bread, but I personally love either a French baguette or cutting into a boule and stuffing it with the garlic and cheese – it looks amazing!

Cut the bread into slices or wedges to suit.

In a small bowl, mix together the softened butter, garlic, Parmesan cheese, dried parsley and some seasoning.

Spread the garlic butter mixture on each slice of bread. Add the grated Cheddar if you want a very cheesy bread.

Place the bread slices in the lined air fryer basket, making sure they are spaced apart, set the temperature to 180°C and cook for 4–5 minutes until golden brown and crispy on the outside.

Remove from the air fryer and serve hot.

Brussels Sprouts with Pancetta & Chestnuts

Serves 4

500g Brussels sprouts, trimmed

2 tbsp olive oil

2 garlic cloves, grated or finely chopped

100g smoked pancetta, diced

100g cooked chestnuts, roughly chopped

1 small onion, diced (optional)

seasoning, to taste

This is a favourite of mine at Christmas, but why wait until then? It is a great side dish for any meal, but when scattered with Parmesan shavings or crumbled feta it could easily become a meal of its own. Try experimenting with different seasonings and spices to create your own unique flavour combinations. Enjoy!

Toss the Brussels sprouts in a bowl with the olive oil, garlic and some salt and pepper.

Add the pancetta, chopped chestnuts and diced onion (if using) to the bowl and mix everything together.

Set your air fryer to 180°C. Place the Brussels sprout mixture in the air fryer basket, making sure it is in a single layer, and cook for 15–20 minutes until they are tender on the inside and crispy on the outside. Shake the basket or stir the mixture halfway through the cooking time so they cook evenly.

Remove the Brussels sprouts from the air fryer and serve hot.

Roasted Cauliflower Steaks

Serves 2

1 head of cauliflower

2 tbsp olive oil

1 tsp garlic powder

1 tsp smoked paprika

1 tsp onion granules

seasoning, to taste

If you haven't tried cauliflower steaks, I urge you to give them a go. These are also delicious when drizzled with a homemade herb sauce (I would use olive oil, fresh herbs, vinegar or white wine vinegar, garlic and seasoning), but you can also add another element by covering them with grated Parmesan – delicious!

Remove the leaves and trim the stem of the cauliflower. Cut the cauliflower into 2.5cm-thick slices, making sure to keep the core intact.

In a small bowl, mix together the olive oil, garlic powder, smoked paprika and onion granules and season well with salt and pepper.

Brush the cauliflower steaks with the seasoned oil, making sure to coat both sides.

Set your air fryer to 190°C, then place the cauliflower steaks in the air fryer basket, making sure they are not overlapping. You may need to cook them in batches. Cook for 10–15 minutes, flipping the steaks halfway through to ensure an even cook. If you want a cheesy crust, you can sprinkle with Parmesan or another cheese and return them to the air fryer until they are browned on both sides.

Check the cauliflower steaks by piercing them with a fork. If they are tender and cooked through, they are ready to serve.

Loaded Jacket Potatoes

Serves 2-4

2-4 baking potatoes

olive oil

4 rashers of smoked bacon
(or 200g pancetta), diced

4 spring onions, sliced

150g mature Cheddar or red
Leicester cheese, grated

seasoning, to taste

I've included this in the side dishes chapter, but loaded jackets can be an amazing meal on their own with some salad alongside. You can add a variety of ingredients to these, but here I've used cheese, bacon and spring onions – delightful! Another of my favourite fillings is swede, carrot and cheese – you must try it. The potatoes can be cooked and stuffed in advance ready the final bake. They can also be frozen.

Scrub the potatoes and pat them dry with kitchen towel. Prick each potato several times with a fork to allow steam to escape, then rub each potato with olive oil, sprinkle with sea salt and place in the air fryer basket, making sure they are not touching each other.

Set your air fryer to 200°C and cook for 35-40 minutes, flipping them halfway through the cooking time.

Check the potatoes for doneness by inserting a fork or skewer into the centre of the potato. If it goes in easily, the potato is done.

Once done, remove from the air fryer. Cook your bacon or pancetta in the air fryer for 4-6 minutes until crispy.

While the bacon is cooking, cut the jacket potatoes in half and scoop out the soft potato. Place this into a bowl with the spring onions, grated cheese and spring onion. When the bacon is cooked, dice and add to the bowl, then season to taste.

When you are ready to cook, place the mixture back into the potato cases and return to the air fryer basket. Cook for another 10-15 minutes until golden.

Serve immediately.

Yorkshire Puddings

Serves 4-6

100g plain flour

2 medium eggs

150ml milk

pinch of salt

1-2 tbsp beef dripping or goose/duck fat (you can use oil, but the fat creates a better flavour)

These are great in the air fryer. You can cook them in small tin foil cases, individual pudding tins (I use 10cm metal tins), or you can use greased ramekins. You can also use this recipe to make giant Yorkshires.

In a large bowl, whisk together the flour, eggs, milk and a pinch of salt until the batter is smooth.

Place ¼ tablespoon of your chosen fat into each of your individual tins (if you are using a large tin, use 1-2 tablespoons). Place in the air fryer and set the temperature to 200°C. Heat for 5 minutes to heat the oil.

Pull out the air fryer basket and carefully pour the batter evenly into the tins, filling each about two thirds full. They will be bubbling and spit a little so do it carefully. Do not overfill as the Yorkshires will rise during cooking.

Continue to cook for 15-20 minutes, or until the Yorkshire puddings are golden brown and puffed up, although the timing will depend on the size of the Yorkshires. You want them to be dry in the middle, not wet. You can also turn them once they are fully cooked to crisp a little more if necessary.

Remove the tins from the air fryer and immediately transfer the Yorkshire puddings to a wire rack to cool slightly before serving.

Rosemary & Garlic Roast Potatoes

Serves 4

1kg Maris Piper potatoes, peeled and cut into chunks

2–3 tbsp goose fat or beef dripping (or use oil if you prefer)

2–3 garlic cloves (left whole)

2–3 sprigs of rosemary

sea salt, to taste

I have been experimenting and found I can prep these roast potatoes in advance and then freeze them. Once steamed, I coat the potatoes in the heated oil, leave them to cool and then open freeze them on a tray, so they are not touching. Once frozen, I then bag them up. Open freezing in this way prevents them sticking to each other. They can then be removed from the freezer and placed into the air fryer basket for easy roasties, although you will need to cook for longer when cooking from frozen.

I love roast potatoes and – without blowing my own trumpet – am pretty well known in the family for my roasties. I have always cooked mine in goose fat in the oven, and, after fluffing them, add semolina to help create a wonderful crispy roastie with a fluffy middle. I was a bit dubious that I'd be able to create the same result in the air fryer as in the oven, but was pleasantly surprised.

Steam or boil the potatoes until they are just starting to soften on the edges slightly.

Meanwhile set your air fryer to 200°C, place your fat into an ovenproof dish and heat in your air fryer for 5–8 minutes until hot.

Drain the potatoes and gently fluff them by placing them back into your dry saucepan and popping a lid on. Shake until it creates fluff around the edge of the potatoes.

Remove the hot fat from the air fryer and use this to cover the roast potatoes. You would traditionally place the potatoes into the hot fat, but as we are air frying, we want to coat them well instead.

Once the potatoes are coated, pop them into the air fryer basket with the garlic and rosemary and cook at 190°C for 30–40 minutes until golden and crisp, shaking occasionally during cooking (the timing will depend on the size of your potato chunks).

Serve with a sprinkle of sea salt. Enjoy!

Mediterranean Roasted Vegetables

**Serves 4 as a side
(or 2 as a main meal)**

1 red pepper, deseeded and sliced

1 yellow pepper, deseeded and sliced

1 courgette, sliced

1 aubergine, sliced

1 red onion, sliced

2 garlic cloves, crushed

8 cherry tomatoes (optional)

1 tbsp olive oil

1 tbsp balsamic vinegar

small handful of fresh oregano, chopped (or 1–2 tsp dried oregano)

2–3 sprigs of thyme
(or 1 tsp dried thyme)

seasoning, to taste

These roasted vegetables are a healthy and delicious side dish but can also make a great main meal if you add some feta and chickpeas to the dish.

In a large bowl, mix all the ingredients together until well combined.

Place the vegetables in the air fryer basket. If you want to keep the juices, it's a good idea to place them in a silicone liner first.

Set your air fryer to 185°C and cook for 10–15 minutes, turning the vegetables halfway through to ensure even cooking.

Serve immediately as a side dish or stir through some chickpeas and feta before serving for a delicious vegetarian main meal.

Pigs in Blankets

Serves 4-6

300g cocktail sausages (approx. 18 sausages)

8-10 rashers of streaky smoked bacon, cut in half

For extra yumminess, you can spread the bacon with a layer of cranberry sauce or wholegrain mustard.

Why do we only have these at Christmas time? They are so yummy, we should really have them more often. You can use any sausage, but I find the small ones work best. These can also be made in advance and cooked from frozen.

Wrap each cocktail sausage with half a rasher of streaky bacon.

Once they are all wrapped, place them into the air fryer basket, set the temperature to 190°C and cook for 10-14 minutes, shaking regularly to ensure they are evenly cooked and crispy.

Serve immediately.

Roasted Broccoli

Serves 4

1 head of broccoli, chopped into bite-size florets

1–2 tbsp olive oil

½ tsp garlic powder

½ tsp onion powder

seasoning, to taste

I love steamed broccoli but roasting it gives it an amazing nutty flavour, which is delightful. This is so easy and makes a change from our standard steamed vegetables. These are also delicious when served with a sprinkle of chilli flakes.

In a large bowl, toss the broccoli florets with the olive oil, garlic powder and onion powder until well coated. Season to taste.

Place the broccoli florets in the air fryer basket, making sure they are not overlapping.

Set your air fryer to 185°C and cook for 8–10 minutes, shaking the basket halfway through to ensure even cooking.

Check the broccoli florets for doneness by piercing them with a fork. If they are tender and slightly charred, they are done.

Serve immediately as a side dish or use as a topping for salads or pasta dishes.

Corn on the Cob

Serves 4

4 fresh corn on the cob

1–2 tbsp butter or olive oil, plus extra to serve

seasoning, to taste

I love corn on the cob, dripping with lashings of butter and black pepper. It is probably the only time in our house where eating with our fingers while having butter dribbling down our chins is not frowned upon!

Brush the corn with butter or olive oil, making sure you coat all sides. Season to taste.

Place the corn cobs in the air fryer basket, making sure they are not touching each other.

Set the temperature to 190°C and cook for 10–15 minutes, turning the cobs every 5 minutes, until the corn is tender and slightly charred.

Serve immediately with lots of butter and black pepper.

8

Desserts

Yes, you can cook desserts in the air fryer – you may just have to be a bit creative if your air fryer is on the small side but if you invest in some small ovenproof dishes and ramekins you should be able to get good results. Ramekins are brilliant in the air fryer and you can get these in different sizes. I have several small ones which are ideal for making your favourite desserts in individual portions, but also have some larger ones that work great if you are cooking for two or three. See page 18 for my tips on safely removing hot ovenproof dishes from an air fryer.

Dietary swaps

We are all becoming increasingly conscious of different ways of eating, whether for health reasons or through lifestyle choices. If you are following a 'standard' recipe but want to make it gluten-free, vegan or sugar-free, here are my top tips to convert any recipe into your way of eating.

Gluten-free

There are some fantastic free-from flours available now – my favourite is from Doves Farm. You can swap like for like with their free-from alternatives and gain great results, though I have found that adding about 30ml (2 tablespoons) more liquid when using gluten-free flour in cakes and sponge puddings gives much better results.

Some dessert recipes contain suet and you can buy gluten-free as well as vegetarian suet now, though you should always check the label before you buy.

Vegan

* You can buy vegan margarines that work as a direct swap for butter. You can also use coconut oil.

* For milk, switch to your favourite plant-based milk (I like almond, coconut or rice milk).

* For eggs, you can buy an egg replacement, but I make my own version by mixing 1 tablespoon of flax or chia seeds with 1 tablespoon of water and leaving to soak for 5 minutes to thicken. You can also use nut butters, stewed fruit, or mashed banana, which can all act as a binder.

* Raw and unsalted cashews are very good for vegan cooking as they can be soaked to form a very creamy base, ideal for desserts or even soups.

Sugar-free

Although this book is not following any diet plan and therefore has no restrictions on fats, carbs, or sugars, many of you may already be aware that I have written several books on sugar-free, low carb and ketogenic diets. I have worked with many schools to reduce sugar intake by 40 per cent in their cakes and desserts, without anyone noticing any changes in flavour. You really don't need things to be super sweet to enjoy them, so please bear this in mind when you are using these recipes.

If you know you have a sweet tooth it's a good idea to reduce the sweetness bit by bit; you will eventually retrain your palate as you become more used to eating fewer sweet foods. Start gradually, allowing you and your family to get used to it, therefore reducing sweet cravings. You can also opt for natural sweeteners that don't spike your blood sugar and are low in fructose, such as erythritol, xylitol, monk fruit granules and stevia. Erythritol also comes as an icing sugar replacement, brown sugar and syrups (known as fibre syrup). You can use stevia in granule or liquid form, but this is over 300 times sweeter than sugar so it can be hard to gauge to taste. If you are reducing your sugar intake, remember that foods high in natural sugars such as bananas, dates, dried fruit, fruit juices, honey, maple syrup, agave, coconut sugar, etc. are all packed with sucrose and fructose, so eating more of these foods is only a sideways step. You will need to cut these down or avoid them entirely in order to keep your blood sugar low. For more information and great recipes, check out my website **www.sarahflower.co.uk**.

Fat

These recipes suggest butter or margarine. I am a fan of butter as I prefer natural foods and butter is not as inflammatory as many man-made fats or seed oils, but you can opt for whatever suits your budget and health objectives.

Fruit Crumble Pot

Serves 1

50–75g mixed frozen berries

1–2 tsp sugar or sweetener
(or to taste)

For the crumble

1 tbsp plain flour

1 tsp butter

1 tsp sugar

2 tsp oats (optional)

This recipe was created because my son loves fruit crumbles. It's really simple and lovely and ticks all the boxes. I use a ramekin dish, but you can use ovenproof mugs if you prefer.

Place the mixed berries into your ramekin dish or mug. Sprinkle with the sugar or sweetener.

Put the flour and butter into a small bowl. Using your fingertips, rub the butter into the flour before adding the sugar and oats (if using).

Sprinkle the crumble onto the berries, then place the mug or ramekin into the air fryer basket. Set the temperature to 180°C and cook for 10–12 minutes.

Serve with a dollop of custard, cream or ice cream.

Chocolate Soufflé

Serves 4

butter, for greasing

1 tbsp cocoa powder, plus extra for dusting

1 tbsp sugar or natural sweetener (or to taste)

3 medium eggs, separated

dusting of icing sugar, to serve

There's no need to be scared of soufflés as they are actually really easy to make. This fantastic recipe uses a very light flourless sponge, making this gluten-free. It is so simple; you just need a hand-held electric mixer, which takes all the effort out of the preparation. These are delicious served straight out of the air fryer with a dollop of cream or ice cream. When cold, they will deflate, but they are still lovely, more like a deflated fatless sponge.

Grease four ramekin dishes or teacups with butter, then dust with a sprinkle of cocoa powder.

Put the cocoa powder, sugar (or sweetener) and egg yolks in one bowl and the egg whites in a separate clean bowl.

Using your hand-held electric mixer, beat the egg whites until they form soft peaks. Leave to one side.

Now use the mixer to beat the egg yolks, cocoa powder and sugar together until they go light and fluffy.

Gently fold a small amount of the beaten egg white into the egg yolk mixture – this helps slacken the mixture.

Carefully add the remaining egg white to the egg yolk mixture and fold by hand very gently, so you do not deflate the egg white. Do not be tempted to mix hard.

Spoon the mixture into your prepared ramekins or teacups, then place into the air fryer basket. Set the temperature to 180°C and cook for 12 minutes.

Dust with icing sugar and serve immediately.

Gooey Lemon Pudding

Serves 4

50g butter, room
temperature, plus extra
for greasing

150g sugar

4 medium eggs, separated

50g plain flour, sifted

300ml milk

1 tsp vanilla extract

zest and juice of 2 large or
3 medium lemons

My mum used to make this pudding when I was a child and I am still addicted to the powerful lemon kick now. This is a wonderfully light pudding, with a delicious and zesty sauce under the light sponge. It works brilliantly in the air fryer, either in individual ramekin dishes, or, if your air fryer allows, baked in a larger ovenproof dish.

Grease four ramekins or one larger ovenproof dish well with butter.

Place the 50g butter and the sugar in a bowl and beat with a hand-held electric mixer until creamy.

Add the egg yolks and beat well before adding the flour and milk and mixing again. Finally add the vanilla, lemon zest and juice to the mixture and combine well. You should have quite a runny batter.

Beat the egg whites in a clean bowl until they form soft peaks, then fold very gently into the lemony batter, being very careful not to overbeat the mixture or the egg whites will deflate.

Spoon the mixture into your dish or ramekins, then place in the air fryer basket. Set the temperature to 170°C and cook for 20–30 minutes (depending on whether you are using ramekins or one larger dish). The pudding should have a golden sponge topping which is firm to touch. This is a saucy pudding, so the centre and bottom will be much softer.

When you serve the pudding, you will notice the bottom half is a gooey lemon sauce and the top should be a lovely light sponge. If you overcook this, it will result in a sponge without the sauce.

Serve with crème fraîche or Greek yoghurt.

Chocolate Bread & Butter Pudding

Serves 4

8–10 slices of white or brioche bread

175g dark chocolate, broken into pieces

80g salted butter, plus extra for greasing

65g caster sugar

3 large eggs

450ml double cream

You can turn this into a chocolate orange pudding by adding some grated orange zest and a few drops of orange extract to the dark chocolate mixture. It is also lovely when the bread is spread with a zesty marmalade. For a boozy extra, you can add a splash of Cointreau or rum to the egg mixture.

This really is the most divine pudding but is not one for anyone watching their waistline – it's so good that you'll almost certainly a second helping. This recipe benefits from being made in advance and left in the fridge until you are ready to cook – it allows the flavours to infuse more to make a delightful dessert. You have been warned!

Grease four ramekins or one larger ovenproof dish well with butter.

Cut your bread slices in half or quarters. These look really lovely when cut into triangles. Place in your ramekins or ovenproof dish.

Put the chocolate, butter and sugar into a heatproof bowl set over a saucepan of just-simmering water to create a bain-marie. Make sure the water does not touch the base of the bowl. You can do this in the microwave but beware as the chocolate can burn very quickly, so do this in 10-second bursts, checking and stirring the mixture in between each burst to check it isn't burning. Stir until the chocolate and butter are melted and fully combined.

Put the eggs and double cream into a large bowl or jug and beat lightly with a fork to combine. Add the chocolate mixture, stirring until fully combined, then carefully pour this over the bread slices. Push the bread down into the egg mixture to help it absorb into the bread. Cover with cling film or foil and place into the fridge for a few hours to allow the bread to soak up the mixture.

When you are ready to cook, set your air fryer to 175°C. Place the dish or dishes into the air fryer basket and cook for 20–25 minutes for individual ramekins, or 25–30 minutes for one larger dish.

Serve with a dollop of cream or ice cream.

Apple & Blackberry Cobbler

Serves 4

3–4 Bramley cooking apples, peeled, cored and cut into chunks

30g light or brown sugar (or less, depending on desired sweetness), plus extra for sprinkling

200g blackberries (or use frozen berries)

For the cobbler mixture

150g self-raising flour

1 tsp baking powder

25g sugar

50g chilled butter, diced

100ml natural yoghurt

1 tsp vanilla extract

milk, for brushing

icing sugar, for dusting

There is nothing more comforting than a lovely apple and blackberry pudding. If blackberries aren't in season you can use frozen blackberries (or try a frozen berry mix) or keep things simple by just using apple with a hint of cinnamon.

Put the apples, sugar and blackberries into a saucepan with 2 tablespoons of water. Cook over a medium-low heat for 5–10 minutes until the apples start to soften, but not completely – you still want them to retain some firmness.

Tip the apple mixture into an ovenproof dish (make sure this fits well in your air fryer; if not, use individual ramekin dishes).

Meanwhile, sift the flour into a bowl, then add the baking powder and sugar. Rub the butter into the flour with your fingertips until it resembles breadcrumbs. Add the yoghurt and vanilla extract and mix until it comes together as a dough.

Now break off large chunks of the dough and place them onto the apple mixture. As it cooks, the chunks will blend together to form a lovely cobbler crust. Or, if you prefer, you can form the dough into a thick sausage and cut it into 3–4cm-thick slices, to form small scone-like circles of dough, and place these artistically onto the apple. When I am in a hurry, I tend to go for the first option.

Brush the tops with milk and follow with a sprinkle of brown sugar, then place in your air fryer basket. Set the temperature to 180°C and cook for 15–18 minutes until the top is lovely and golden.

Dust with icing sugar and serve.

Chocolate Saucy Pudding

Serves 4

115g butter, room
temperature, plus extra
for greasing

115g sugar

2 medium eggs, beaten

2 tbsp milk

1 tbsp vanilla extract or
vanilla bean paste

100g self-raising flour

2 tbsp cocoa powder

For the sauce

300ml boiling water

2 tbsp sugar

1 heaped tbsp cocoa powder

icing sugar, for dusting

My mum used to make this when we were children, and I rediscovered the recipe when I was looking through her personal cookery notebook. We used to call this a magic pudding as the sauce is poured over the top of the cake, but during cooking it miraculously goes to the bottom. It works brilliantly in the air fryer, either in ramekin dishes, or, if your air fryer has enough room, baked in an ovenproof dish.

Grease four ramekins or one large ovenproof dish with butter.

Put the butter and sugar into a bowl and use a hand-held electric whisk to beat them together until creamy and fluffy. Gradually add the beaten eggs, milk and vanilla and mix well before adding the flour and cocoa powder and mixing until it forms a thick batter.

Pour the batter into your prepared ramekins or ovenproof dish and smooth over until flat.

In a bowl or jug, mix the boiling water, sugar and cocoa powder together and stir thoroughly until dissolved and lump free. Pour this over the sponge mixture.

Place in the air fryer basket, set the temperature to 165°C and cook for 20–30 minutes (depending on the size of your individual dish) until the sponge is firm to touch.

Dust with icing sugar and serve with a dollop of cream or crème fraîche – enjoy!

Rice Pudding

Serves 4

750ml whole milk

80g pudding rice

3 tbsp sugar

1 tbsp butter, plus extra
for greasing

2 tsp vanilla bean paste

200ml double cream

grating of nutmeg

jam, to serve

Yes, you can cook rice pudding in the air fryer, but don't try and rush things or you will end up with rice that is tough and chewy. I prefer to start things off in a saucepan before adding the rice to an ovenproof dish or ramekins as I find this really improves how they bake and speeds up the process. For an alternative flavour, why not try adding the seeds from 15 crushed green cardamom pods along with the sugar and using coconut cream instead of double cream? If you are vegan, you could also use vegan butter and swap the milk for coconut milk and add a carton of vegan cream to create a creamy consistency and flavour.

Grease four ramekins or one large ovenproof dish with butter.

Pour the milk into a saucepan along with the rice and sugar, then add the butter and vanilla.

Place over a low-medium heat and cook for 10 minutes, stirring regularly, until it is simmering. Add the cream and remove from the heat.

Pour into your ovenproof dish or ramekins. Sprinkle with the grated nutmeg and cover with foil, securing tightly.

Set your air fryer to 170°C, then place the rice pudding dish or dishes into your air fryer basket and cook for 30–35 minutes. If you're cooking in ramekins, you will need to adjust the cooking time to 20–25 minutes. Check halfway through cooking and give it a stir, as there will be patches of thick rice gathering at the edges.

Remove the foil and stir well. If the rice is too thick, add more milk or cream, and if it is not soft enough, cook for another 10–15 minutes.

Serve with a generous dollop of jam.

Chocolate Fondant

Serves 4

125g dark chocolate, broken into pieces

100g butter, room temperature, plus extra for greasing

130g sugar

3 large eggs

1 tsp vanilla extract

60g plain flour, sifted

icing sugar, for dusting

Who can resist a chocolate fondant? The gooey centre is divine but is only achieved if you don't overcook the sponge, so timing is everything. As you get to know your own air fryer, you will be able to gauge this more accurately. I would suggest for your first attempt it is better for this to be cooked slightly under than over.

Grease four individual ramekin dishes well with butter.

Place the chocolate in a heatproof bowl and set this over a saucepan of just-simmering water to create a bain-marie, making sure the water does not touch the base of the bowl. You can do this in the microwave but beware as it burns very quickly, so do this in 10-second bursts, checking and stirring the mixture before the next 10-second burst to ensure it does not burn. Stir until the chocolate is melted and fully combined.

Use a hand-held electric whisk to beat together the butter and sugar until light and fluffy. Add the eggs and vanilla and combine well before folding in the flour.

Finally, add the melted chocolate and combine well, then pour in the mixture into the ramekins. Place these into your air fryer basket, set the temperature to 185°C and cook for 8–10 minutes until they are spongy to touch but soft in the middle.

Remove the ramekins from the air fryer and turn each one out onto a serving plate. Sprinkle with icing sugar and serve with a dollop of ice cream and some fresh raspberries – delicious!

Mini Ricotta Cheesecakes

Serves 4

8–10 chocolate digestive biscuits, crushed

50g butter, melted

300g ricotta cheese

75g sour cream

2 medium eggs

100g icing sugar

zest of 1 large lemon

2 tsp vanilla bean paste

To add a burst of lemon flavour, simply add the zest of 2–3 lemons to the mixture. When cooked and cooled, drizzle over some lemon curd.

These are so lovely and yet so easy to make. I use a silicone pudding mould for this, but you can use silicone cupcake moulds or the larger silicone muffin moulds. You can also make these in ramekin dishes, but they can be difficult if you want to turn them out before serving – glass dishes look much better. I have topped mine with some raspberry coulis, sliced strawberries and a drizzle of chocolate sauce but you can top them with whatever you prefer.

Put the crushed biscuits into a bowl, add the melted butter and stir to combine.

Place 2–3 teaspoons of this mixture into each of your mini cheesecake moulds or ramekins. Press down to form a firm base.

Add the ricotta cheese, sour cream and eggs to a bowl and combine thoroughly. Add the icing sugar, lemon zest and vanilla bean paste and combine again.

Spoon the ricotta mixture into your moulds/ramekins and spread to create an even top.

Set your air fryer to 165°C, place the cheesecakes into the air fryer basket and cook for 15 minutes until they have started to set. Remove from the air fryer and allow to cool before chilling in the fridge.

When ready to eat, decorate as desired.

Blueberry Clafoutis

Serves 4-6

300ml double cream

25g butter, plus extra
for greasing

1 tsp vanilla extract or vanilla
bean paste

2 medium eggs, plus
3 egg yolks

120g sugar

50g ground almonds

1 tsp baking powder

70g plain flour, sifted

150g raspberries or
blueberries

I love a good clafoutis but these flavours in particular are to die for! Serve with a dollop of extra-thick cream or ice cream for a really delicious dessert.

Grease your ramekin dishes with butter.

Heat the cream, butter and vanilla in a saucepan over a low heat until the butter has melted (do not let it boil). Remove from the heat and allow to cool.

Using a hand-held electric mixer, beat the eggs, egg yolks and sugar together in a bowl until light and fluffy. Add the ground almonds, baking powder and flour to the egg mixture and combine well, then gradually add the cream mixture to form a batter. You can use a balloon whisk to ensure it is all mixed well.

Place the berries in the base of your ramekins, then pour the cake batter over the berries. Don't worry if the berries bob up, that is fine.

Place the ramekins into your air fryer basket, set the temperature to 170°C and cook for 20 minutes, or until firm. If the tops are browing too much, turn the heat down.

Serve immediately with cream or ice cream.

9

Sweet Bakes

You can bake in the air fryer as if it were a conventional oven but the main drawback is lack of space. A single air fryer with a small basket is not going to fit any standard cake tin or oven dish, so you have to learn to improvise. I have put my suggestions below so do read these before you venture into air fryer baking. It will ultimately save you lots of time and failed attempts.

BROWNIES

Yes, you can make these in the air fryer. Much depends on the size of your air fryer basket and the size of the cake tin you use. A 20cm tin will fit most larger models of air fryer and obviously with the mini ovens, cake tins can go larger. If you have a small air fryer, you can cook brownies in batches in smaller tins or use a silicone liner.

CUPCAKES

I love making cupcakes in the air fryer. I have tried both the air fryer mini oven as well as the basket and both work well. To cook cupcakes in a basic air fryer basket, I highly recommend using silicone cupcake cases lined with paper cases as this helps the cupcakes retain their shape but are also better for handling when cool.

DIETARY SWAPS

For tips on making these sweet bake recipes suitable for gluten-free, vegan or sugar-free diets, see pages 186–187.

Chocolate Brownies

Makes 4–6

115g butter, melted, plus extra for greasing

200g sugar

2 large eggs

1 tsp vanilla extract

60g plain flour

50g cocoa powder

½ tsp baking powder

60g chopped walnuts (optional)

Who doesn't love a chocolate brownie? This very simple recipe works well in the air fryer. If you like a very gooey middle, reduce the cooking time by 5 minutes. I love to serve these hot with a chocolate sauce and a dollop of cream but they are just as good cold, with a cup of tea or coffee.

Grease or line your baking tin, making sure that it will fit in the air fryer basket.

In a large bowl, whisk together the melted butter and sugar until it is light and well combined.

Add the eggs and vanilla extract to the bowl and whisk until the mixture is smooth.

Sift in the flour, cocoa powder and baking powder and combine well, then fold in the chopped walnuts (if using).

Pour the batter into the prepared tin and then place in the air fryer basket. Set the temperature to 175°C and cook for 20–25 minutes, or until firm to touch. If you want a gooey middle, cook for 5 minutes less.

Remove from the air fryer and allow the brownies to cool (if you like) before cutting into squares.

Palmier Puffs

Makes 10–12

1 sheet of ready-to-use puff pastry

60g butter, melted

2–3 tbsp brown sugar

1–2 tsp ground cinnamon

1 egg, beaten

Palmier Puffs are a type of pastry that can be cooked in an air fryer for a delicious and crispy sweet snack. They look so lovely, like little hearts, and are so simple to make. You can also vary the recipe by spreading the pastry with jam, chocolate spread or lemon curd.

Unroll the puff pastry sheet out onto a lightly floured surface.

Brush the pastry rectangle with the melted butter. Mix together the brown sugar and cinnamon, then sprinkle this over the pastry, ensuring it is evenly covered all over.

Starting at one of the long edges, roll the one side of the pastry into the centre, the roll the other long side to the centre so that both rolls meet. You should be left with 2 sausages of pastry, joined in the middle.

Using a sharp knife, carefully cut the double roll into 10–12 slices, approximately 2cm thick. Place each slice, flat side down, onto a tray or worktop. These should look like little hearts. Brush each piece with beaten egg.

Place the Palmier Puffs in the air fryer basket, leaving space between each one to allow for air circulation and because they will expand slightly as they cook. You may have to cook in batches depending on the size of your air fryer.

Set the temperature to 180°C and cook for 15 minutes, or until the Palmier Puffs are golden brown and crispy.

Remove them from the air fryer and let them cool before serving, though they are also delicious warm!

Chocolate Cupcakes

Makes 6

110g butter, room
temperature

100g granulated sugar

2 medium eggs

70g plain flour, sifted

1 tsp baking powder

40g cocoa powder

These are great to experiment with in your air fryer and you can guarantee everyone will love them. They are amazing with a thick swirl of chocolate ganache on top, or just drizzled with a melted chocolate, although you can also just keep them simple. Enjoy!

Line six silicone cupcake cases with paper cupcake liners.

In a large bowl, cream together the butter and sugar until light and fluffy.

Add the eggs one at a time, mixing well after each addition, and beat until well combined. Add the sifted flour, baking powder and cocoa powder and fold gently until combined.

Fill each cupcake case two thirds full of the cake mixture, then place them into the air fryer basket, ensuring they do not overlap and are not too overcrowded.

Set the temperature to 175°C and cook for 12–15 minutes, or until a toothpick inserted into the centre of a cupcake comes out clean.

Once the cupcakes are done, remove them from the air fryer and let them cool completely before frosting and decorating as desired.

The Best Scones

Makes 6 scones

100ml buttermilk

1 medium egg

250g self-raising flour, plus extra for dusting

50g chilled butter, diced

50g sugar

50g dried mixed fruit

1 tsp mixed spice (optional)

flaked almonds (optional)

a little milk, for brushing

Really, these are the best scones. I have used this recipe for years and even used this when teaching children: despite them overworking the dough, all the scones turned out brilliantly. It is foolproof, and the secret is in the buttermilk. You will never use another recipe again!

Lightly beat the buttermilk and egg together in a jug and leave to one side.

Put the flour and butter into a bowl and, using your fingertips, rub the butter until it disappears into the flour. It should look a little bit like breadcrumbs.

Add the sugar, dried fruit and mixed spice (if using) and stir well before adding the egg and buttermilk mixture. Stir with a wooden spoon until it forms a dough.

Sprinkle a little flour onto your board and tip out the dough. Using your hands, knead the dough before flattening out to 3-4cm thick.

Cut the scones, either using a round cutter or with a knife into six circles, squares or triangles. If you like, sprinkle on top with flaked almonds. Place into the air fryer basket – you may need to do this in batches if you have a small air fryer.

Set your air fryer to 180°C, then brush the scones with a little beaten egg or milk (I often add a little milk to the empty jug of egg and buttermilk). Bake for 10–12 minutes. The scones should be just starting to turn golden – you don't want to overcook them, so don't wait until they are brown!

Remove the scones from the air fryer and let them cool before serving them with cream and jam.

Apple Turnovers

Makes 6

1–2 cooking apples, peeled and diced

1–2 tbsp sugar (or to taste)

1 sheet of ready-to-use puff pastry

1 egg, beaten

1–2 tbsp soft brown sugar (optional)

flour, for dusting

No one likes a soggy bottom, so if you are using wet ingredients in the turnover, as in this recipe, do check the bottoms of the turnovers. If they are not as brown as you would like, turn them over and cook for a few minutes more for an even, crisp pastry.

Apple turnovers are so simple to make and always delight. You can change the recipe to suit – why not add some cinnamon and dried fruit, or you can use jam, lemon curd or even Nutella for a twist on this recipe.

Place the diced apple into a saucepan with 1–2 tablespoons of water and the sugar and cook gently over a low-medium heat until the apple starts to soften. You want a mixture of soft and chunky apple which is not too wet. Remove from heat and leave to cool.

Unroll the puff pastry sheet onto a lightly floured surface, then cut the puff pastry sheet into 6 equal squares.

Spoon a small amount of the apple onto one side of each puff pastry square. Do not overfill or the apple will spill out.

Brush the edges of the pastry with a little beaten egg, then carefully fold the pastry squares in half to create a triangle, pinching the edges together to seal in the filling.

Use a fork to gently press down on the edges of the pastry to create a decorative pattern, then brush each turnover with beaten egg and finish with a sprinkle of brown sugar (if using).

Place the apple turnovers in the air fryer basket, leaving space between each one to allow for air circulation and ensuring they do not overlap. You may need to cook these in batches depending on the size of your air fryer.

Set the temperature to 190°C and cook for 15–20 minutes, or until the turnovers are golden brown and crispy.

Remove the turnovers from the air fryer, dust with flour and serve hot or cold.

Chocolate Chip Cookies

Makes 8–10

110g butter, room
temperature

130g soft light brown sugar

2 large eggs

1 tsp vanilla extract

220g plain flour

30g cornflour

1 tsp bicarbonate of soda

200g dark chocolate chips

My son loves chocolate chip cookies, so it was one of my first experiments in the air fryer. Suffice to say, they turned out brilliantly and have become a firm favourite. They will need to be cooked in batches, unless you have a larger air fryer or an air fryer oven, or you can halve the recipe quantities to make fewer cookies.

Cream together the butter and sugar in a large bowl until light and fluffy.

Add the eggs one at a time, beating well after each addition, then stir in the vanilla extract.

Gradually add the plain flour, cornflour and bicarbonate of soda to the wet mixture and mix until just combined. Finally fold in the chocolate chips.

Line your air fryer basket with a paper liner or a silicone liner. This is very important as the cookies will stick if placed directly into the basket.

Grab a small amount of dough and form into a ball approximately 3cm in diameter. Place this into the lined air fryer basket. They will spread when cooking, so depending on your air fryer, I would bake just 3 or 4 at a time (the mixture makes 8–10 cookies), spacing them out evenly.

Set the temperature to 160°C and bake for 10–12 minutes, or until the cookies are golden brown on the outside and still soft in the middle.

Remove the cookies from the air fryer basket and let them cool on a wire rack before placing in an airtight container.

Lemon Cupcakes

Makes 6

125g butter, softened

150g sugar

2 large eggs

180g self-raising flour

1 tsp vanilla extract

2 tbsp lemon zest

juice of 1 lemon

½ tsp baking powder

I love the zesty kick of a lemon cake – citrus is a perfect match to the sweetness. These are so easy and delicious. I like mine served with a dollop of yoghurt and a handful of berries, but you can make a buttercream, or if you have some lemon zest and lemon juice left over, you can make them into lemon drizzle cupcakes, pouring some of the juice over the cupcakes 5 minutes before the end of the cooking time and again when cooked.

Line six silicone cupcake cases with paper cupcake liners.

Cream together the butter and sugar in a large bowl until light and fluffy.

Add the eggs one at a time, beating well after each addition and alternating with a small amount of the flour – this stops the mixture curdling.

Mix in the vanilla extract, lemon zest and lemon juice.

Gradually add the remaining flour and the baking powder and fold in until just combined.

Fill the cupcake cases about three-quarters full of batter, then place them into the air fryer basket, ensuring they are not touching. Set your air fryer to 175°C and bake for 12–15 minutes, or until a toothpick inserted into the centre of a cupcake comes out clean.

Once the cupcakes are done, remove them from the air fryer and let them cool completely on a wire rack before storing in an airtight container.

10

Savoury Bakes

This chapter features delicious savoury items that are perfect for snacks, lunches, simple suppers or as part of a buffet-style spread. It shows how versatile the air fryer really is – this is why I urge you all to think of this machine more as an oven than a means to fry food without oil. I use puff pastry in a few of these recipes, but shortcrust would also work: I use shop-bought pastry for ease, but you can certainly make your own if you have the time.

All pastry recipes will freeze brilliantly. I freeze mine uncooked: simply place on a baking tray in the freezer, then when frozen remove and transfer freezer bags. This way they won't stick together, so I can then pull out however many I want and bake when needed. This is also a great time-saving way to get ahead for events such as Christmas, because your freezer can be full of your favourite treats. I do this every year with my mince pies – I freeze them in silicone baking trays, pop them out when frozen, and then place them back into the baking tray when I am ready to bake. Perfect for when I have impromptu visitors who are often in awe when I produce fresh bakes without breaking a sweat!

Pizza Pinwheels

Makes 8–10 pinwheels

flour, for dusting

1 sheet of ready-to-use
puff pastry

1 jar sundried tomato paste

2–3 slices of ham, torn into
strips

100g mature Cheddar cheese,
grated

1 tsp dried oregano

1 egg, beaten

small handful of sesame seeds
(optional)

seasoning, to taste

**My son loves these – when he was little they were one of
the main things he had in his packed lunch. You can, of
course, choose any filling to suit, which is what makes
them so versatile. They also freeze brilliantly, so you can
make a batch, freeze them uncooked, and just pop them
out of the freezer whenever you fancy them.**

On a lightly floured work surface, unroll the puff pastry – you
should get a rectangle that is approximately 30cm x 20cm.

Spread the sundried tomato paste evenly over the pastry,
leaving a 1cm border around the edges. Season with salt
and pepper.

Add the ham, ensuring it is evenly distributed. Follow this with
the cheese, oregano and more salt and pepper.

Starting at one of the long edges, fold or roll the pastry in on
itself slightly to start. Continue to roll until you end up with one
long sausage. Push the ends in to tidy up the shape as
sometimes these can splay out a little.

Cut the roll into 8–10 equal pieces, approximately 2cm in
thickness, and place them, cut-side down, on a lined or
greased tray.

Brush the pinwheels with beaten egg followed by a sprinkle
of sesame seeds (if using).

When ready to cook, set your air fryer to 180°C. Add the
pinwheels into the air fryer basket – you can place a piece of
baking parchment on the base if you want to prevent any
possible sticking issues. Ensure they are not overlapping, and
they have a little room to spread and puff up. You may have to
do these in batches depending on the size of your air fryer.

Bake for 15–20 minutes, or until golden brown. Serve warm or
leave to cool.

Kale Crisps

Serves 2

1 bunch of kale, washed and dried

1 tbsp olive oil

seasoning, to taste

grated Parmesan cheese, garlic powder or other seasoning of your choice (optional)

As a nation, we all love crisps, but they are not the healthiest snack. Kale crisps, on the other hand, are a great healthy alternative and are surprisingly tasty. This is a basic recipe so do experiment with different flavourings.

Remove the kale leaves from the tough stems and then tear them into bite-size pieces.

Toss the kale leaves into a large bowl with the olive oil, salt, pepper and any other seasonings you like.

Arrange the seasoned kale leaves in a single layer in the air fryer basket, making sure they are not overlapping.

Set the temperature to 160°C and cook the kale crisps for 5–6 minutes until they are crispy and golden brown. You may need to shake the basket or flip the leaves halfway through the cooking time.

Gorgonzola & Spinach Puffs

Makes 6

flour, for dusting

1 sheet of ready-to-use
puff pastry

75g baby leaf spinach

120g Gorgonzola cheese,
crumbled

1 egg, beaten

6 walnuts (optional)

small handful of sesame seeds

seasoning, to taste

These look amazing despite requiring so little effort. That is the joy of ready-to-go puff pastry! Just like the other savoury pastry recipes in this chapter, they are perfect for lunches, buffet-style celebrations or light dinners served with a delicious salad.

On a lightly floured work surface, unroll the puff pastry – you should get a rectangle that is approximately 30cm x 20cm.

Cut into 6 squares, each roughly 10cm x 10cm.

Place the spinach leaves into a colander or sieve and run under hot water until the leaves start to wilt. Squeeze the spinach in some kitchen towel to remove any excess water.

Divide the spinach between each pastry square, adding it to the centre of each one.

Add equal amounts of the Gorgonzola to each square – take care not to overfill and leave a clearly defined edge around each. Season to taste.

Pull each corner of the square up and over into the centre and push down. You can use a little of the beaten egg to help it hold if you need to. If you want to be really fancy, you can place a walnut into each centre, but this is entirely optional.

Once you have completed all the squares, brush with beaten egg followed by a sprinkle of sesame seeds.

Add the pastries to the air fryer basket – you can place a piece of baking parchment on the base if you want to prevent any possible sticking issues. Ensure they are not overlapping, and they have a little room to grow. You may have to do these in batches depending on the size of your air fryer.

Set the temperature to 180°C and bake for 15–20 minutes, or until golden brown. Serve warm or leave to cool.

Cheese & Bacon Scones

Makes 6–8

100ml buttermilk

1 medium egg

250g self-raising flour, plus extra for dusting

50g chilled butter, diced

75g cooked smoked bacon, diced

4 spring onions, finely diced

100g extra-mature Cheddar cheese, grated

½ tsp chilli powder

seasoning, to taste

milk, for brushing

Always make the scone to the thickness you want them to be once baked. So many people expect scones to double their size when cooked (they don't) and then get disappointed when their scones end up flat and unattractive.

These make a great alternative to bread and are absolutely delicious. You can make them as traditional-shaped scones using a round cutter, but I prefer to cut them into triangles – they look so much nicer in my opinion. I love them with lashings of butter or some crumbled blue cheese and a dollop of chilli marmalade, but you will find your own favourites.

Lightly beat the buttermilk and egg together in a jug and leave to one side.

Put the flour and butter into a large bowl and, using your fingertips, rub the butter until it disappears into the flour. It should look a little bit like breadcrumbs.

Add the bacon, spring onions, cheese, chilli powder and salt and pepper to taste. Stir well before adding the buttermilk and egg mixture, then stir again with a wooden spoon until it forms a firm dough.

Sprinkle a little flour onto your board and tip out the dough. Using your hands, knead the dough lightly before flattening out to 3–4cm thick.

Cut the scones into your desired shape and place into the air fryer basket. You may need to do this in batches if you have a small air fryer.

Set the temperature to 180°C, brush the tops with a little beaten egg or milk and then bake for 10–12 minutes. The scones should be just starting to turn golden – you don't want to overcook them, so don't wait until they are brown!

Remove the scones from the air fryer and serve warm.

Savoury Cream Cheese & Salmon Pinwheels

Makes 8–10 pinwheels

flour, for dusting

1 sheet of ready-to-use puff pastry

100g garlic and herb cream cheese

100g smoked salmon, thinly sliced

1 egg, beaten

seasoning, to taste

These are great for a lunch, snack or buffet-style meal, served hot or cold. They keep in an airtight container in the fridge for several days, but they are very moreish, so are unlikely to last that long. So simple to make, you will wonder why you have never made them before.

On a lightly floured work surface, unroll the puff pastry – you should get a rectangle that is approximately 30cm x 20cm.

Spread the cream cheese evenly over the pastry, leaving a 1cm border around the edges. Season with salt and pepper.

Arrange the smoked salmon slices evenly over the cream cheese, overlapping them slightly.

Starting at one of the long edges, roll or fold slightly to start. Continue to roll until you end up with one long sausage. Push the ends in to tidy up the shape as sometimes these can splay out a little.

Cut the roll into 8–10 equal pieces approximately 2cm in thickness and place them, cut side down, on a lined or greased tray. Brush the pinwheels with beaten egg.

Set the temperature to 180°C and add the pinwheels to the air fryer basket – you can place a piece of baking parchment on the base if you want to prevent any possible sticking issues. Ensure they are not overlapping, and they have a little room to grow. You may have to do these in batches depending on the size of your air fryer.

Set the temperature to 180°C and bake for 15–20 minutes, or until golden brown. Serve warm or leave to cool.

Puffed Sausage Rolls

**Makes approx.
10 sausage rolls**

2 sheets shop-bought
puff pastry

flour, for dusting

500g sausage meat

1 tsp dried thyme

½ tsp dried oregano

1 small onion, very finely
chopped

1 egg, beaten

sprinkle of sesame seeds
(optional)

seasoning, to taste

*For a variation, why not put a
layer of your favourite chutney
or pickle onto the pastry
before adding the sausage
meat?*

**This sausage roll recipe uses puff pastry, but you can use
shortcrust if you prefer. The joy of this recipe is you can
use whatever sausage meat you prefer. I like to use
good-quality gluten-free sausage meat as it contains
more meat and less fillers and does not create as much
fat leakage. You can also use chicken sausages (just cut
them out of their skins) or even vegetarian ones. I like to
add herbs to mine to jazz them up a little, but you can
keep it simple if you prefer.**

On a lightly floured work surface, roll out the puff pastry to
a rectangle that is approximately 30cm x 25cm. Cut this
lengthways into two, so you end up with two long but wide
rectangles.

Add the sausage meat, herbs and onion to a large bowl and
season with salt and pepper. Combine well until evenly mixed.

Grab half the sausage meat and form into a long sausage to fit
the length of your pastry. Place this into the centre of one of
the pastry rectangles. Brush each side of the pastry with the
beaten egg.

Starting with one of the long edges, roll the pastry over the
sausage meat to meet the other edge. Push down to form a
good seal. I normally have a little edge to seal and then roll over
this to help secure. Push the ends in to tidy up the shape as
sometimes these can splay out a little. You can trim off any
excess pastry if necessary.

Cut the roll into five equal pieces, approximately 5cm each.

Brush the sausage rolls with beaten egg and finish with a
sprinkle of sesame seeds (if using). Repeat with the remaining
sausage meat and the other piece of pastry.

When you are ready to cook, add the sausage rolls to the air fryer basket – you can place a piece of baking parchment on the base if you want to prevent any possible sticking issues. Ensure they are not overlapping, and they have a little room to puff up. You may have to do these in batches depending on the size of your air fryer.

Set the temperature to 180°C and bake for 20–25 minutes, or until golden brown. You can turn these once the top is cooked if you have a soggy bottom (sometimes this can happen with meat with a high fat content).

Once cooked, remove from the air fryer and serve hot or leave them to cool and store in an airtight container.

Index